BABY BOOMER BACHELORETTE

or,

How to Have Sex at Least Once More Before You Die

♀

First Edition

BABY BOOMER BACHELORETTE

or,

How to Have Sex at Least Once More Before You Die

♀

Patsy Stagner

JPS Publishing Company

BABY BOOMER BACHELORETTE
or,
How to Have Sex at Least Once More Before You Die

By Patsy Stagner

Published by: JPS Publishing Company
P.O. Box 540272
Grand Prairie, TX 75054-0272 U.S.A.

Library of Congress Cataloging-in-Publication Data

Stagner, Patsy.
   Baby boomer bachelorette, or, How to have sex at least once more before you die / Patsy Stagner.
   p. cm.
   Includes bibliographical references and index.
   LCCN 2003115494
   ISBN 0-9664924-4-7

   1. Man-woman relationships--United States. 2. Dating (Social customs)--United States. 3. Baby boom generation--United States--Life skills guides.   I. Title. II. Title: How to have sex at least once more before you die

HQ801.S73 2004   306.73'0973
                                   QBI33-1722

DISCLAIMER

This book provides information regarding the covered subject matter. Neither the publisher nor the author is engaged in rendering legal, medical, accounting, psychiatric or psychological, or other professional advice. If expert assistance is needed, the services of a professional should be sought.

This book does not contain all the information that is available on this subject. For more information, see the references in the *Further Reading* section.

The sole purpose of this book is to entertain. There may be mistakes both typographical and in content. The author and the publisher have no liability or responsibility to any person or entity with respect to any loss or damage caused, or alleged to be caused, directly or indirectly, by the information in this book.

If you do not wish to be bound by the above, you may return this book to the publisher for a full refund.

ABOUT THE AUTHOR

Patsy Stagner is a Baby Boomer who becomes upset when she hears other Baby Boomers say they're old. She seethes when anybody tries to write them off as over-the-hill, insignificant, or asexual. She believes we're in our prime when we reach so-called middle-age and is determined to prove it. This book is calculated to make Baby Boomers rebel against the status quo, to enable men and women in their forties and fifties to realize dreams they thought were over for them, and to reach a level of fulfillment they never dreamed possible.

She lives in a suburb of Dallas, Texas with her dog, Cookie, and her cat, Blossom. She's written award-winning short stories, a soon-to-be-published novel, and has co-written a diet and exercise book.

She plans to date until she's 100, or until there are no men left on earth who will go out with her–whichever comes first. She credits her thriving love life to following her own suggestions—the suggestions detailed in *Baby Boomer Bachelorette or, How to Have Sex at Least Once More Before You Die.*

Visit her website at www.patsystagner.com.

TABLE OF CONTENTS
♀

Postproduction:

PREPRODUCTION
♀

Introduction

I hadn't been exactly dateless for the past ten years, but they'd been as scarce as chips on the porcelain in Martha Stewart's cupboards.

Did being closer to fifty than forty have anything to do with it? I didn't like to think so, but the truth is somewhere out there. I thought I looked pretty good for my age. But when you have to start adding the phrase "for my age," you know the men aren't queuing up at your front door like the paparazzi after Ben and J. Lo.

I've never liked to use the word "desperate" in relation to my ability to attract men. In fact, I've never had to use it. And even though it might be appropo in this moment of my life, I refuse to use it now.

So, for the record, it wasn't desperation that led me to place a personal ad in the local paper. Curiosity, yes, that was the right word.

It didn't take long for me to begin a correspondence with three eligible bachelors.

Bachelor Number One sent a photograph of himself giving the thumbs-up sign to the picture-taker from the cockpit of a Cessna Citation. I love a man with a hobby, so I shot back a response telling Number One I really liked his airplane. His reply stated he no longer had it. Disappointed, I said I was sorry. Did he no longer enjoy flying? He said the Citation had been repossessed along with his Lexis, Yukon, and Harley. Not to worry, though, he still had transportation. He could meet me anywhere I wanted on his Schwinn. I declined the invitation and told him I had gotten back with my old boyfriend.

Bachelor Number Two informed me he was an animal lover. That made me ecstatic. I immediately wrote him back and told him that I, too, loved animals. In fact, I had three mutts rescued from death row at the pound, and they, along with two cats, all slept with me at night. I never heard from Bachelor Number Two again.

Bachelor Number Three appeared to be a good match. He sent a black and white photograph taken at the health club in his apartment building that showed him pumping the chest press machine. I spent a small part of my week at the YMCA, so we at least had that in common.

We arranged to meet at the coffee shop at the Barnes & Noble in Arlington. I arrived a little early and hid among the book shelves. I planned to spot Number Three when he first walked in, just to be prepared. His description said he had dark hair, blue eyes and was of average height.

There he was. Since when does five-feet-five inches qualify as "average" height for a man? No place to run, he had spotted me.

"Hi." He smiled. He wasn't missing any teeth.

I smiled back. I wasn't missing any teeth either.

Give the guy a break. Everyone can't be Brendan Fraser. I stood next to Number Three as we ordered our coffee. The top of his head was level with my eyes. I felt sure I could take him, all that working out notwithstanding.

Make the best of it. He's not that bad. It could have been much worse. He's college-educated, has a good job, and his height might not be a problem for another woman. Give him a chance.

"You don't like to drink caffeinated coffee?" He removed the lid from his Cappuccino Frappe Grandé and took a sip.

I stared at his hands. Small, white and smooth, they belonged to a porcelain doll. That's why I quit dating lawyers (one of the reasons, anyway). I don't like a man's hands to be softer than mine.

"Caffeine keeps me awake at night." I stirred two packets of artificial sweetener into my White Chocolate Mocha Venté decaf.

"I like to drink caffeine and take ephedra at the same time. Gives me tremendous energy."

"Not to mention severe heart palpitations."

He laughed and looked into my eyes. Uh oh. I suspected he might be falling in love.

Number Three told me about his three ex-wives, and I smiled and nodded sympathetically at each sad tale. I only had one ex-husband to compare with Number Three, but I felt like good old Norman could hold his own with any ten ex-wives. A boozing, womanizing out-of-work fence builder held up well against ex-wives who merely grew bored and left.

Grew bored and left. Those words bounced around in my brain while Number Three droned on. Then a man sat down at the next table. Dark brown hair hung over his shoulder in a limp ponytail. His mustache hadn't been trimmed since the Reagan Administration, and worn, torn jeans with a tie-dyed T-shirt looked like props from "That 70's Show." He tossed his head and used a hand with bitten fingernails to push his ponytail back. Number Three and I stared. The Twenty-First Century hippy was the most interesting thing going on in the room.

The hippy looked right at me. He gazed with curiosity at first, then the light of recognition flashed in his eyes. He leaped from the table, marched over, pushed a thin hand toward me. I took it without thinking. We shook hands with gusto.

"Long time, no see," the hippy said. He studied my face, his brown eyes aglow.

I couldn't say anything and was afraid to look at Number Three.

"Have you been over there lately?" The hippy still looked at me intently.

"Over there?" I said.

"The group? Have you been to the group lately?"

I studied the hippy and thought I recognized something under the hair and mustache. "What's your name?"

"I'm Colin."

"Colin!" I leaped from the table, ran around and hugged him. "I'm so happy to see you." I still didn't look at Number Three. The silence coming from his side of the table was deafening. I sat back down.

"Maybe you didn't recognize me because of the hair," Colin said.

"The last time I saw you, you didn't have any." I gave a nervous laugh. I didn't turn my head, but looked at Number Three out of the corner of my eye. He stared transfixed at Colin.

Colin looked benignly at Number Three. "I had a brain tumor. Taking radiation, so all my hair fell out." Colin smiled pleasantly. Number Three said nothing.

"Are you okay now?" I asked, "It's been awhile."

"I'm fine." Colin must have felt uncomfortable leaving Number Three out of the conversation. "We knew each other from a group we both attended," Collin said to Number Three.

"What group?" Number Three spoke at last.

Colin looked as if he wanted me to tell him it was okay to continue. I kept my face neutral. He hesitated, then plunged ahead. "A support group for people who've been abducted by aliens."

I spat White Chocolate Mocha onto the table. After I stopped sputtering, I said, "Well, it's good to see you again, Colin. Glad you beat it."

Colin reached out, took my hand and shook it. Then he reached for Number Three. I thought Number Three might pull away, but he allowed Colin to shake his hand too. Colin walked away into the book store. I wondered what books he intended to buy.

One of those proverbial pregnant silences followed his departure. I stirred my coffee and waited for Number Three to ask. Surely anyone would want to know what that had all been about. If I had been in Number Three's position, I would have asked immediately who that guy was and what was he talking about. Of course, I'm the type who thinks if I want to know it, it's my business.

Apparently, other people in the world were too polite to ask personal questions. Number Three glanced quickly at me, but was unable to sustain lengthy eye contact. "Would you like another coffee," he finally asked.

I was dying to explain the exchange between me and Colin, but I refused to volunteer the information. Number Three was going to have to ask. He never did. The evening continued as if Colin had never happened. Number Three even invited me to a jazz club later. I said I had a breakfast appointment, so couldn't stay out that late. Number Three walked me to my car, and we parted amicably. I never heard from him again, and I canceled my personal ad.

All Number Three would have had to do was ask. I would have been happy to tell him Colin and I were members of the same group of Alcoholics Anonymous, and the reason Colin made up that story about being abducted by aliens was to avoid breaking AA's anonymity code.

It didn't bother me, however, that there was someone in the world who thought I had been abducted by aliens. Sometimes, I thought so too.

***

When it comes to over-forty dating, if you feel like you've been abducted by aliens, taken to another planet, and dropped into a reality for which you were totally unprepared, then stay tuned for the following production of *Baby Boomer Bachelorette* and learn a better way.

1. A Cause Looking for a Rebel

Ever read something in a book that sounds true, or sounds as if it should be true, but a niggling doubt still hovers? Maybe you even want it to be true, because it sounds so reasonable and rational, but somehow you just can't swallow it?

Much of the advice you receive about dating is like that. One of the purposes of this book is to do some myth-busting. Among those myths: the necessity of self-esteem; everyone who claims to have a sense of humor really has one; you should never tell a lie; the existence of the vaginal orgasm; and the desirability of making love all night. Stay tuned to witness these and many other dating and sex myths busted!

I hesitate to use the word "advice," because that's not necessarily what I'm doing. My goal is to share the knowledge I gained through research and personal experience. I'll pass on the tips and warnings I gathered from interviewing peers who have first-hand, over-forty dating experience. We're going to explore some of the things that prevent us from going for

everything we desire in life, and learn how to overcome many
of those obstacles. It's up to you to put into practice the things
you learn here, but only if they make sense to you.

Herd of Baby Boomers

There is a herd of rarified creatures born between the
years 1946 and 1964. These "Baby Boomers"—perpetually
youthful, successful and never satisfied with accepting
traditional roles—roam every state of the United States. The
U.S. Census Bureau reported that of the 97 million Americans
who are forty-five or older, almost 40% are single. Of this
ubiquitous group, according to a recent American Association
of Retired Persons (AARP) study, 60% of singles ages forty to
sixty-nine are women.

When we were teenagers, dating was a traumatic phase
that we went through, then got over. Oceans of words were
written to guide us through it. Now that we are Baby Boomers,
there is little information to help us. Dating for us means facing
a Texas tornado without a storm cellar, and we're desperately
looking for something to make it the easy, happy and fulfilling
experience we know it should be. We're willing to do it, but
we're scared to death.

Old at Fifty?

Seventy-six-million Baby Boomers are turning fifty at
the rate of one every 7.5 seconds, and we think, or we've been
told that, our lives are over—the best part of it anyway. If we
are old at fifty, as we're being told by our friends, family, the
media, and health care professionals, it would mean we're

going to be spending *half of our lives being old*. Do you feel old, look old, or act old? I don't!

At a family gathering, I listened carefully to what my relatives were saying. Two cousins, both barely in their sixties; my aunt, in her seventies; and another not yet fifty, talked about how old and decrepit they were becoming, identifying themselves as somebody's grandmother, and describing in colorful detail their various and sundry ailments. They intimated that we were all getting old, and this was to be expected.

"I'm not old," I informed them. "I'll let you know when I am." I intend to live to be one-hundred-fifty. I won't even consider myself middle-aged until I'm seventy-five.

The first time we say, "I must be getting old," we are giving ourselves permission to acquire a whole slew of characteristics and attributes we would formerly have looked upon as undesirable, unattractive and even comical. If we tell ourselves we are old, or allow our friends and family to tell us, our minds begin to believe it. If our minds believe it, our bodies believe it. We become cranky, slow-moving, lazy, absent-minded and reluctant to try new things. Every time we forget the name of the movie we just saw, or our knees crack when we climb the stairs, or laugh so hard we pee in our pants, we blame it on our age. Remind yourself that these things happen to everyone, and shouldn't automatically be blamed on age.

Always challenge anybody who makes ageist remarks, or treats you like an old person. If we allow these things to go uncontradicted, we are giving implied consent. Let those around you know that you do not intend to go quietly into senility, that you are going to fight it all the way. You expect their support, not their condescension.

On the average, people live twenty years after retirement, and this number is increasing all the time. As Baby Boomers, we could be looking at thirty or forty years of retirement. Do you really want to spend all of those years sick, diseased and old? Just after the age of fifty, I caught myself thinking: "This may be the last home I'll ever own. I'll probably never buy another new car. The way things are now is the way they're going to be until I die. There will never be anything else for me."

That threw me into a major panic. The thought of it being all over, that there would be nothing new to look forward to, made me sick to my stomach. I had plans, and aspirations, and dreams. I didn't want it to be over—ever!

Endless Life, Endless Possibilities

Then the next logical thought arrived in my over-stimulated brain: *Nobody knows when they're going to die.* Regardless of how long the average life expectancy is, there's no way to predict how long a person will live. That makes my life open-ended. With endless life comes endless possibilities. I could have a dozen new cars. I could have a house on the top of a mountain in Colorado, or two or more husbands, if I wanted. I could write the Great American Novel at the age of one hundred. What was there to prevent me? Who would stop me? No one, except myself.

Even though I had reached forty, fifty, sixty or seventy, I didn't have to start the march to death. I didn't have to count down the minutes or hours until the end. I could live each day as if it were my last—which everyone should be doing anyway—knowing full well it wasn't. That is, while I prepared myself legally and financially for the future, I was truly living one day at a time, each one to its fullest potential, never assuming this was the end.

I had no excuse to sit in my rocking chair, watching TV and marking the days off my Mr. Winkle calendar (see www.mrwinkle.com) until I died. I could do anything, go anywhere, be whatever I wanted to be. I was alive, now and forever, if I wanted to be. As long as I thought it in my mind, it was so.

Life at Forty or Fifty is Just Beginning

People who grew up in the fifties and sixties, as Baby Boomers did, were told how to live their lives by authority figures. We respected authority and thought anyone in such a position must have the right answers. Fathers, preachers, teachers, doctors, scientists, anyone who had attained a certain position of prestige and power, were to be admired and obeyed. Despite our rebelliousness in the sixties—that was just a small minority of the vast hordes of Baby Boomers—we settled down to conventional lives, and did, for the most part, what we were told was the right thing to do.

Suddenly, we turned fifty and were told it was time to look forward to retiring. We had been good little boys and girls, but would no longer be needed in the work force. There were younger people for whom we had to make room, and they would do our jobs for us. We were to be relegated to gated communities, retirement homes or assisted living facilities. There we could challenge our minds with endless rounds of bingo and identify ourselves with our stumbling, bumbling contemporaries who complained about their numerous illnesses and died with astonishing regularity. Every day we would be reminded of those in our peer group—senior citizens—who had "passed away." We couldn't even utter the forbidden word out loud: *died*. No one really died, they merely "passed" into another sphere, and we whispered their names with reverence and fear.

Baby Boomers aren't ready to be told the second half of their lives doesn't count! We refuse to be put out to pasture until we pass away!

Starting Over

Now is our time to start over. To begin fresh. Many of us are free from the constraints of nine-to-five jobs; our families are raised and no longer need us in the same way; we are free to do whatever we want. It's as if we were newly born infants, freshly scrubbed and powdered, who still retained all the knowledge we laboriously gained over many years of living. Everything familiar is new and exciting again. We can wake up in a different world, and it's a beautiful one with endless possibilities. We are in charge of our own lives, and don't have to compromise.

Remember the things we used to do when we were unselfconscious children? We ran without fear of falling. We swam without looking for snakes in the river. We blew bubbles and chased after then, bursting what we had created. We made farting noises until our companions collapsed with giggling. We jumped rope until we were breathless, and laughed with reckless abandon.

Recently, I took my dog walking to a nearby park. On a whim, I sat in a swing and pushed myself off. As I began to swing higher and higher, a feeling of excitement grew in the pit of my stomach. It felt like the first time I took a jeep trip over

Black Bear Pass in the Colorado Rockies. Fear, exhilaration, and longing meshed together as I held my breath and swung as high as the swing would take me. For those few minutes, I felt completely joyful, ecstatic with total self-abandonment. No worries, no tension, no inhibitions. I flew.

We can recapture that feeling of youth, only better. We can have the spirit of youth, but the wisdom of age. We can have it all, but we have to change our mind set.

Midlife Stresses

Boomer women are faced with many stressful situations. They may be trying to balance work and family, and many feel as if they're working too much. The divorce rate is rising like a flooding river, and job stability is an oxymoron. On top of all that, we are having to care for the young and the elderly while trying to cope with our own changing bodies and health problems.

Midlife Not a "Crisis," But an Opportunity

Even women who have taken care of themselves by eating right, exercising and using anti-aging products begin to notice that their bodies are changing despite their efforts. It's easy to see what is happening on the outside. The challenge we face is to consider what is happening inside our heads. Now is the time to review options, of which they are many, and make decisions about our futures. We have reached the middle of our lives (most of us), and now is the time to change what has been troubling us.

Our middle years should not be seen as a crisis, but as an opportunity for a new adulthood. We only have one, very short childhood, but we can have two adulthoods, maybe more. Now is the time to reinvent ourselves. Many Baby Boomer women are seeing midlife as a creative opportunity. They are writing books and making movies and creating websites about their experiences. They are sharing them with other women in the same situation.

We Have to Rebel!

We have to rebel the way many of us did in the sixties. Even if you were never part of a love-in, or a ban-the-bomb protest, or a desegregation march, now is the time to make up for it. Hold up your banners that read, "I am Young," and "I'll Never Retire!" even when all those around you are succumbing to the myths of old age. *Protest* when somebody refers to anyone over forty as being old. *Never* let anyone get away with making you an old coot or a granny. You're spirited, you're vibrant, you're amazingly alive in a way you have never been before.

We live in a liberalized society, but we refuse to allow ourselves to take advantage of it. We are still constricted by what we were taught when we were growing up, when we believed what those authority figures were telling us. Now they are trying to tell us we're old. Do not believe it.

I'm not suggesting that anyone throw off their moral beliefs, or shirk their responsibilities. I'm just saying that there are no limits, except the ones we place on ourselves. Abandon your old ideas and take on new ones.

We can exercise, eat right and take supplements to stay healthy, but the key to remaining young is in our minds. Associate yourself with those who are as young-hearted as you are. If you don't know anyone like that, then all the more reason to seek out someone who shares your attitude. That's why we want to find another Baby Boomer as our companion. We want to live, love and be happy!

Close your mind to those who would try to bring you down, or make you act or look a certain way based on their perception of what a person your age should be like. Do it even if it is your kids, or your significant other, or your parents, or even your doctor. Rage against the dying of the light.

Rebel!

2. The Concept

I'm sure many readers of this book watched the series "The Bachelor" and "The Bachelorette." The success of those shows spawned countless others like, "Date Patrol," "Average Joe," and "Joe Millionaire."

Why are those programs so spellbinding? Human beings are endlessly fascinating. Add to that the competition, the glamour, and, most importantly, the romance, and you have an irresistible mix. Romance is a universal favorite and appeals to everyone. You can call it sex, love, or infatuation, but the fact remains that most people are either in love, have been in love, or want to be in love. Homo sapiens have the nesting instinct. It's even true of men, the confirmed bachelor George Clooney notwithstanding. And even he sleeps with his pot-bellied pig.

Even when the nest isn't a permanent one, we relish the feeling of belonging to someone and of someone belonging to us. We like to create a barrier around that relationship that protects it from the rest of the world. We feel as if we are unique and special, and there is certainly no one else like our beloved.

Baby Boomers Need and Desire Romance

It's been proven over and over again that when we are engaged in a happy and fulfilling romantic relationship, we are less depressed, less likely to become addicted to drugs, alcohol, food or anything else. People involved with the opposite sex in an intimate way even live longer. You can't beat that result.

Romance gets our juices flowing, our hormones flare into action. We are the stars of our own production, succumb to the Julia Roberts syndrome, and fall in love with our leading man (or lady). When we're alone, without someone to love, we long for the feeling again. If we've lost the one we love, whether through breakup or death, we become fearful of losing another loved one. We are reluctant to try again, to put our feelings on the line, to take the chance on being hurt. This becomes especially true as we age. We feel as if we have lost the power to attract someone of the opposite sex like we did in our youth. We still have those feelings—the longing, the excitement, the sexual need—but our fear increases proportionally with our age.

Fear was keeping me from doing something I longed to do, from finding the companion I desired. We Baby Boomers might not look as good in a bikini as those young women on "The Bachelorette." But even if we didn't have the physical attributes we had in our youths, we had so very much more.

I began to think of my search for someone to share my life with as a reality program called "Baby Boomer Bachelorette—the Miniseries." I was the producer, the director, the scriptwriter and the star. I placed myself in charge of all aspects of the production. It could be anything I desired as long as I carefully planned and executed the program. I made my search a game. Not a life-or-death situation, but an opportunity to have fun. As a result, the whole process was less dreadful and scary.

My "concept" for the program was that I, a Baby Boomer, with perseverance and a plan, could find sex and love again. And if I could do it, anybody could.

Preproduction Stage

Every television broadcast begins with "preproduction." It's the most important part of the program. If I researched and planned carefully, I believed I could create a successful one myself that accomplished what I wanted it to. The goals of the production were the goals of this book: to venture into the scary world of Baby Boomer dating, share my experiences with others, and teach them how to succeed. We want our production to create a desire in our audience to take some action. We want the opposite sex of the species to notice us and want to pursue a relationship with us. But if we don't know where we're going, how will we know when we've arrived?

The Talent

First, we needed to get the "talent" whipped into shape. That talent was me, and I desperately needed help. In bad movies about Hollywood, they have to throw the hero or heroine into rehab and get them ready for the production. That's what needed to be done for me (not rehab—I'd already done that years ago), but a complete overhaul. A mere makeover wouldn't do. I had to be revamped from the inside out. Could it be done? Was there time before I was so far gone I couldn't be fixed?

Just before I turned forty, I quit smoking. It was September 29, and by Thanksgiving of the same year, I had gained twenty pounds. I had merely substituted food for cigarettes. (This is a whole other subject, addressed in my book, *Fit, Fifty and Fabulous*, to be published later this year.) Shortly after that, my boyfriend of two years dumped me for no apparent reason. Not one that was apparent to me anyway. I lost what little self-confidence I had and gained more weight. I was fat, forty and faceless, because no one sees an overweight, middle-aged woman. They are invisible. I could have walked into a bank, robbed it at gunpoint, and no one would have been able to pick me out of a line-up of other over-weight, middle-aged women.

I stopped caring about myself—my clothes, my hair, my makeup—and stopped thinking of myself as a sexual person. Believe it or not, this went on for ten years. I felt too depressed and powerless to change anything. I felt disconnected from life. (There were other mitigating factors besides the weight gain and the boyfriend loss, but they're not relevant to this book.)

I'm not the only one having these kinds of feelings. Many women are facing life crises as they approach middle age. Julie*, a divorcee for many years, has grown children who will not accept responsibility and leave home. Melinda has a son facing manslaughter charges in a drinking and driving accident. Often we face poverty because our husbands left us. Cynda is becoming a grandmother with a teenage daughter who still lives

---

*Not her real name. The names of all the people I interviewed for this book have been changed.

at home. Some of us gained weight for the first time after menopause. We lost energy and our hair fell out. We may be bored with our long-time jobs and are stressed from lack of challenge, fulfillment or appreciation.

What can we do?

Stop Blaming Others

First, I stopped blaming others. The way I felt wasn't the fault of my ex-boyfriend. It wasn't the way strangers overlooked me. It wasn't that my boss didn't appreciate me. Even if those things were true, the way I felt had nothing to do with others or anything outside of myself. It's too late to fix your husband, your boss or your kids. *I was my problem, and I was my solution.* The cliche that the only thing you can change is yourself is a cliche because it is true. I could have become depressed thinking about all I might have accomplished over those ten years. Instead, I chalked them up to experience and let them go. I gathered up my remaining strength, determined to grab every new opportunity that presented itself. If none did, I would create my own.

The images we see on the media—TV, magazines, movies—make us think everyone is better looking, thinner, happier and richer than we are. An award-winning writer is credited with saying that's why we have fiction. It sounds like a contradiction, but fiction exposes us to reality, and shows us people who are just like us, flaws and all.

Stop Clinging to the Past

In the present, single Baby Boomers are all looking for the same things, but we cling to people and events from our pasts. We must start living in the moment. As we age, we tend to look back and romanticize the past. Our first kiss was the best we've ever had. We will never find anyone like our first love, or our dead husband, or the perfect boyfriend who dumped us for no apparent reason.

Embrace change. Nothing is ever going to be the same as it was before. But that's good. In fact, it's great! It's like starting over in a new world with endless opportunities and possibilities.

What's Going on Inside?

We can easily see what's going on outside ourselves. Our formerly perky breasts may be sagging a bit, or a deep frown line might furrow our forehead, and our abdominals aren't washboards as they once were. But what's going on inside? That's the big question. If I had been checking into my mental progress as I aged, I wouldn't have had to hit bottom before I did something about it. I'm not very good at assessing my inner self. When I hit bottom, I landed with a heavy thud, a blow that knocked me unconscious. When I emerged from the coma, I was ten years older, fifty pounds heavier, and too self-conscious and weary to even think about associating with the opposite sex in a romantic way.

Spending time working on ourselves is a good investment. You probably spend more time maintaining your home than you do maintaining yourself. Even if we only live to the United States's average life expectancy, we still have thirty or forty more years of life. Do we want to spend that time overweight, sluggish, sick, disabled and alone? It's not necessary, and is imminently preventable. But you have to be a rebel, rage against the status quo, and don't believe what other people tell you about growing older. Decide what being a so-called middle-aged person means to you, and act accordingly. You're scripting your own production. Don't allow someone else to write the future for you.

Self-Assessment

It is important to assess who we are now, what kind of person we are on the inside. We can build on that and make plans for being the kind of person we want to be in the future. If we don't know who were are, how are we going to know what kind of person we are looking for?

Make a list of all the things about your life that don't work. Now, you have a choice to make. You can continue to ignore them, or, if you can't ignore them, learn to live with them. The best choice, the ONLY choice in my book, is to resolve to change them. Remember—your life is an open-ended block of time. You have the time to change anything that isn't working, and you can choose how you want to spend the next forty years.

Possibly you are someone who avoids challenges and change because you might suffer some discomfort? Is your life really so wonderful that you can afford to continue on the same way? Change does take some effort, which is why most people never attempt to change unless some cataclysmic upheaval makes it necessary. Once you make a small change, however, take one small step, it gets easier. When you see the difference these changes make in your life, you begin to embrace change as a part of life, a desirable event that you look forward to. Hard to believe, I know, but just do it, and you'll see.

Once you make the choice to change, you gain control. That's the difference between making the change voluntarily and not because you have to. You're in control. Life is by its very nature in constant flux. You can fight it, and be disgruntled by it, or you can go with it, harness it, and mold the final product into the shape you desire.

Believe you deserve everything you want, because that's the first step in attaining it. A program on the Travel Channel, counted down the best ways to win in Las Vegas. One way was to believe with every fiber of your being that you were going to win. Psych yourself up to win. A trainer showed a gambler how to work himself up into believing he was going to win, and by the time he made it to the casino, he was bursting with self-confidence. He began to win round after round of blackjack. He inspired the woman sitting next to him so much that she began to believe she was a winner too. Soon, she began to win. The gambler left the tables with piles of money he hadn't arrived with.

You're a winner, and I'm a winner. It's time the rest of the world found out about it.

I asked myself one question, which was the beginning of my pursuit for all the sex and love to which I was entitled.

What would it take to make me happy?

3. What Would It Take to Make Me Happy?

We've come up with our concept. Our bachelorette is going to get herself together and find sex and love. But she's in bad shape right now. She has much work to do before we begin the actual production. Can't have a successful program without our starlet functioning at her peak and feeling self-confident. How do we do that?

The first thing I asked myself was, "What Would It Take to Make Me Happy?" I love lists, so I wrote the things I thought of, not necessarily in order of importance, but just as they occurred to me. The final list looked like this:

1. A spiritual relationship with a power greater than myself;

2. Excellent health and a body I wasn't ashamed of;

3.   Make money doing something I love doing;
4.   A feeling of connectedness with my loved ones; and
5.   A relationship with a member of the opposite sex.

Compose one of your own. It may be slightly different from mine, but probably not much. Human beings seem to have the same basic needs and desires.

Learn to Put Yourself First

In order to make our heroine, our star, our "talent," the winner we know she is, we have to make her believe it. Many Baby Boomers need to get over feeling guilty when we do something for ourselves. Although our generation has been condemned as self-indulgent pleasure-seekers, the truth is that we spend more time on others than we do on ourselves, especially women.

Woman have found themselves walking a tightrope. We want and expect to be career builders, and we want and expect to be great mothers. We want and expect to be perfect wives and companions. Unfortunately, it's not humanly possible to be perfect at all of these things all the time. As a consequence, time for ourselves goes out the window as we struggle to balance the other aspects of our too-busy lives. No wonder so many women suffer from anxiety and depression! We're trying to do too much, and it's impossible. We blame ourselves. We feel guilty and exhausted. We take drugs to give us more energy and to make us feel better. It usually doesn't work, because it doesn't address the fundamental problem.

We Need More Time

Mostly, we just don't have enough time. If you made a list of all the things you did during the course of a day, a week or a month, could you find something that could be eliminated or adjusted so you could make time for yourself? How about watching television? I watch at least three hours of television a day, and much more on the weekends. Once that television clicks on, I'm hypnotized. I won't be leaving my easy chair except to get food or drinks during the commercials. Regardless of whether there is anything worth watching on or not, I'll sit and mindlessly press the remote buttons, lingering for a few seconds on one program, then moving quickly to the next. Don't kid yourself. You do the same thing.

If I expect to get anything done, I have to leave the TV off. Period.

Hire somebody to clean your house—a big time waster as far as I'm concerned. Think about it. Wouldn't it be more productive if you spent your time elsewhere? Hire a mowing service to do your lawn. All of this if you can afford it, of course. But be honest. Many people refuse to hire a maid or lawn service because they feel guilty having someone do it for them, or they don't want a stranger in their house, or they don't think the cleaning is good enough. These are control issues, and they are robbing you of the life you deserve. "Milking the mouse," it's called. Don't sweat the small stuff.

I don't remember who all has a key to my house—my maid, my ex-maid, the pet sitter, my cousin—and none of them have ever taken anything from it. Get over whatever is stopping you. Let go of the money, and use your time more productively. Spend more time with your kids or grandkids; find a great date; finish your income tax return so you can get that refund; work on your home-based business so you can quit working for someone else at a job you despise.

How about sleeping, cooking, eating, driving to and from work or children's activities? Can you car pool or take public transportation and do something constructive while someone else is driving? If you must drive, how about listening to self-help or inspirational audio tapes while you do your errands? Give it some thought, and I'll bet you can come up with a little extra time to spend just on yourself.

Now that we have freed up a few hours, let's concentrate on the things that need to change.

Choose to be Happy

Every self-help guru emphasizes that we can choose to be happy. It's not something that materializes from nothing. It's a choice we make. I suppose that's true, as long as you don't have some sort of chemical or psychological reason for your depression, and even then, there's always help from outside sources.

Wearing life like a loose garment is always good advice, but it's not as easy as it sounds. Is it really possible to shrug off the daily frustrations and disappointments without letting it effect our sense of well-being? Acceptance comes naturally to some people. With little effort, they are able to let go of things over which they have no control. I wish I were that kind of person. I wish I could automatically let the fool who's driving slower in the HOV lane than the motorists in regular traffic go about his leisurely pace without wanting to throttle him. It would be great if I didn't fantasize about gearing up my Honda and passing him on the short-lived HOV shoulder, waving a sign that reads "MORON!" in big, black letters.

Whew! My heart rate shot up while I typed those sentences on my computer. It's imperative that we put these kinds of situations in their proper perspective. If the regular traffic is moving faster than the HOV, I shouldn't have entered the HOV. Regardless, I'm going to make it home within five minutes of what I regularly do anyway, so what's the difference? It's not as if I won't be home in time to watch "The Bachelorette." So calm down. As my sister often tells me, "You're not going to a fire." Listen to relaxation tapes in your car, or calming music, or a book-on-tape. Forget about the traffic, and use the time to your advantage. Think about a pleasant trip or plan a dinner menu.

Develop your own personal happiness plan. It could be simple or complex. You could be making preparations to completely change your life or merely change its day-to-day aspects. You may have resolved to smile at a neighborhood child, say a kind word to your boss (they rarely receive appreciation), or buy lunch for a good friend you haven't seen in a while. Simple things easily accomplished by anybody.

However, our Baby Boomer Bachelorette doesn't just want to change a few things. She is in dire need of a complete overhaul. She has been neglecting herself for ten years, and that takes a vicious toll on her physical health, physique and mental health. We have a lot to do before we can get her into shape for the big show.

Let's begin with what is going on in her mind. If we can get her head screwed on straight, we can expecting her body to follow.

Before I focus on our starlet, however, permit me to deviate for a moment.

4. Our Biggest Fear

U rban legend suggests that our biggest fear is speaking in public. We are more afraid of it than we are of dying. Since I don't have that particular fear—except the one about dying—I believe we have an even greater fear than public speaking. An unacknowledged one. One you don't even know about, and you're going to hate me for exposing. It's . . . drum roll . . . the *fear of change*!

I've tried to analyze why people are so afraid of changing, why at the mention of lifestyle changes, everyone immediately says, "I could never give up . . . (cigarettes, alcohol, you-fill-in-the-blank)." Even if it might mean an extension of one's life for several years, not to mention freedom from disease or discomfort, we are unable to break through our inertia and make the lifestyle changes necessary to overcome a certain predilection.

I doubt if even the psychiatrists and psychologists could explain why the majority of us are unable to change. But the minute you mention that something in a person's life might not be working, and suggest some much needed renovations, the defenses immediately go up.

You would think a life-altering and incredibly painful disease like cancer would force a person to change their lifestyle, but it doesn't seem to. Doctors and scientists are telling us in increasing numbers to eat more fruits and vegetables, because there's strong evidence that they protect you from cancer. Nobody I know is doing it. How about you? Are any of your friends or family following this advice? Are you?

We Have Choices

Part of the problem with changing is that we don't realize we have choices. We have always done things a certain way—usually the way our parents did them—and we cannot imagine another way. We are enclosed within the restrictions of what we can see or what we've previously experienced, and find imagining another course impossible. To begin, we must imagine what our lives would be like if we made a certain change. Then, taking one step at a time, we move inch-by-inch, easing closer to our boundaries. We break through those barriers, cross over our self-imposed constraints, and fly away like eagles soaring above the Grand Canyon.

Imagine Another Way

A recent Discovery Channel program portrayed the ascent of man. The development of the species was predicated upon the imagination of a particular group. The world was in flux or change, just as our world is today. The group of prehistoric creatures who were able to imagine living in a different world in a different way were the ones who survived. They were able to picture themselves adapting to walking on their hind legs. The other future-human variations could not. Imagination is what saved the species, not power or maintaining the status quo.

Uncertainty plagues those of us who want to change. We want to go back to the easy way, the way we've always done it, back to the place where we feel comfortable. We experience inertia, depression, hopelessness. We are like humans in the movies who are bitten by werewolves. Our hands and faces begin to sprout hair, our changing skeletal structure cracks and breaks, and claws shoot from the tips of our fingers and toes. Eventually, we come to realize that discomfort is the first signal that we are beginning to change. In the next scene, the full-blown werewolf is howling at the moon.

We can embrace the discomfort by controlling the direction we are taking. We have a certain goal in mind, have imagined a different life. We determine what steps are needed to attain our goal, one in which we walk on our hind legs. We believe with our entire being that it is in our best interests to reach that goal. Our faith that we can make it happen lessens the discomfort, and we are ready to face the unknown, heedless of our fear.

Worst Case Scenario

I like to ask myself what the worst case scenario is. What's the worst thing that could happen? If I go on a diet, I won't be able to eat chocolate cake. If I can't eat chocolate cake, I will die. Therefore, I must eat chocolate cake. I can't stop myself from eating it. I am a weak, spineless person who is a victim of her addictions. What I am really saying is that I'm afraid to go on a diet because I might fail. This has been reinforced in my mind, because I have failed many, many times before. Why should this time be any different?

Fear of Failure

What about all the other times I've attempted to change something and failed? I tried countless times to quit smoking. After many failed attempts, I finally succeeded. Those failures were merely the steps it took to get to the point of success. Failure is the building block upon which success is achieved. The only difference between you and the successful dieter is that they have failed enough to get them to the success place. How many times do we have to fail before we hit the heights of success? You won't know the answer to that until you reach it. It's different for every individual and every situation.

Fear of the Unknown

Some people are afraid of the unknown. They believe they are happier with a predictable life. But let's be honest. No life is predictable. Things happen all the time over which we have no control. The unknown can be exciting, exhilarating. We are heady with anticipation while we strive to reach our goals. Maintaining the status quo is highly overrated. We should shake things up at every opportunity.

One warning, though. Change is a process, sometimes slow, sometimes fast. Each and every action taken to initiate change is important in itself. It should be savored, studied and thought about. Don't rush through the process like you would a cold shower. When you have taken the last step and hit the top rung of success, sit for a minute and savor it just as climbers summiting Everest exhilarate at the top of the world's tallest mountain. When your breath returns, set another goal.

Stay in the moment. You have heard that phrase countless times, but if you spend too much time looking forward, you will never savor what's happening in the present. That's all there really is anyway. If you are so caught up in the goal, you won't be able to notice the friends, family and fun surrounding you, and you'll miss out.

Don't Set Impossible Goals

Sometimes, we set a goal, like losing weight, and decide that as soon as we've reached that goal, we'll be happy. We will go on the Internet and search for a date as soon as we've lost ten pounds. After we lose ten pounds, we decide we are still not thin enough, so we change the goal to ten more pounds. We are using our inability to reach perfection as an excuse not to start looking for a companion. I quit using imperfection as a way of putting off life. As soon as you reach one goal, there will be another one to work on. Life is constantly changing, whether we want it to or not. You're the one who's in charge of your own destiny when you take control of the changes rather than merely allowing them to happen.

My friend at work said she thought I was happy the way I was, that I was comfortable with my life and didn't have room in it for someone else. I had to concede that she was partly right. I pointed out, however, that unlike many people, I recognized that I had a problem. That's the first step in changing anything. Second, that I was willing to change. Willingness is the key that opens the door to change.

We have set our goal of producing a successful dating plan and putting it into execution for our Baby Boomer

Bachelorette. We're going to have fun in the process, and we're going to enjoy every step that leads to our record-breaking program.

Let's see where our bachelorette is right now.

5. Fear of Dying

In my discussions with female Baby Boomers, fear of dying was not at the top of their list. Even though we may have lived half our lives, many of us are apparently okay with our mortality.

An Unexamined Life

Letty Cottin Pogrebin, in her book *Getting Over Getting Older*, believes the American obsession with youth may command so much of our attention, that it forces us to leave unexamined the "human condition." That is, the diminishing of time and the inevitability of death. We are focusing on the exterior, while not allowing ourselves to examine how it feels to age, or what our fears are regarding our mortality. We neglect to notice the important details or closely observe the passage of time from the point of view of our aging.

I would like to briefly address dying, even though many of us neither like nor feel it necessary to think about it. I feared this natural phenomenon, and was forced to examine my fears regarding it when I consulted a psychologist. She said I suffered from "existential anxiety." I can sum up this problem in a few words which will be easier to understand than the literature I've read that describes it.

Existential Anxiety

"Existential anxiety" is the inability to accept life on life's terms. This also includes difficulty accepting the inevitability of death. We may be able to distract ourselves with the details of day-to-day living, and never give it a thought. But some of us wake up in the middle of the night with a panic attack, the reality of our death a cold shadow hovering above our heads.

I complained to my psychologist about the injustices of the universe, and asked how could there be a loving god who cared about and watched over us when there was so much suffering in the world? Then, after years of abject suffering, we were going to die. There was no justice. The innocent suffered mercilessly. What was the meaning of it all? What was the point in even getting up in the morning when it could end at any moment? America's concentration on youth had not deflected me from worrying about my mortality.

When I'm above tree line, at the top of a fourteen thousand foot mountain in Colorado, I'm happy and feel spiritually connected. But when I watch the Discovery Channel, and see animals killing and eating each other, I am plunged into despair. When I watch the news on TV or read the newspaper, I see raping, murdering, natural disasters, terrorism. I feel depressed, can't sleep at night and wake up with a feeling of despair. I don't have the answer to this universal dilemma, with the exception of suggesting you not watch or read the news.

If you suffer from this, all I can offer are a few suggestions about how I managed to come to terms with this phenomenon.

This is important because I—our heroine—needs to find some sort of relationship with a power greater than herself, or she will be completely dysfunctional in this so-called unjust world. In fact, it's number one on her "What Would It Take to Make Me Happy?" list. How can I be happy, she wonders, when all I feel is anger and powerlessness?

Turn Anger into Action

Rage is, indeed, a negative emotion, but anger can be turned to our advantage. Who doesn't feel anger and righteous indignation when they see the weak, the helpless and the small brutalized and taken advantage of? There are lots of things to be angry about, which shows a passion and honor for life, and it can be a catalyst for change.

Whatever you may believe in the way of faith, be sure it is respectful of all life. If you believe something that hurts or destroys others, then it's time to reconsider.

Many of our beliefs come from authority figures. Priests, rabbis, pastors, gurus, mommy, daddy or the President all seem to know something we don't. They've attained a level of importance in the world to which we feel we could never aspire. We rationalize that what they tell us must be the truth, or else how would they be in a position of authority? Surely god must be speaking through them.

This is what I was talking about earlier that is a Baby Boomer problem. Worshiping authority is a habit we learned early in life, during the fifties and sixties. The world was a much less complicated place then. Incredible scientific discoveries, apparent harmony between parents (fewer divorces), and relative prosperity made it seem as if what we were being told was the truth. Everything was rosy, wasn't it? Why rock the boat?

We feel more insecure in matters of faith than almost any other area. Making our own choices there seems patently conceited, and we feel we must have a higher authority interpret and intercede for us. We need someone more knowledgeable and scholarly to tell us what it all means. We are afraid to contact whatever higher power we seek directly, lest we be deemed upstarts and blasphemers, even if that higher power is to be found inside ourselves. We must have some sort of intermediary telling us what to do, the way to do it, and when's the best time to do it.

Please don't think this is an indictment of religious faith and rituals. Not at all. I'm just seeking to convince Baby Boomers to think outside the box, to trust themselves, and to find their own meanings.

Ask yourself what the consequences of your beliefs are, how it affects you and other people, how it affects the natural world. For example, I realized that the inertia created by my anxiety prevented me from being of use to anyone. My fear of dying enervated me, and kept me from finding meaning in anything. My existence seemed pointless, and I felt as if I served no useful purpose.

Acceptance

The key to most things in life you are unable to change is acceptance. Things are the way they are, whether we like them or not. Even though I didn't agree with the way the process of life was set up—nobody asked my opinion—I chose to accept it on its terms. There wasn't anything I could do about it anyway. I could either accept it and go on to find some meaning, or I could be miserable the rest of my life. Or, I could end my life. The obvious choice was acceptance.

Find Meaning in Life

That didn't keep me from seeking meaning, however. I picked a cause I felt strongly about, and proceeded to try to make a difference in that arena. I wanted to help animals. To further this cause, I contribute money to animal organizations. Pick something you believe strongly in, whether it's your church, the environment or child advocacy, and work for it.

Inevitability of Death

My fear of dying was another matter. I'm amazed when people say they're not afraid to die. I used to be petrified at the thought, and couldn't understand why others weren't. I'm definitely in the minority on this matter.

Then, I bought fifty acres of land on a lake. What possible difference could that make?

In Texas, if you don't want to pay property taxes on land at the residential rate, you have to obtain an agricultural exemption. One way you can receive the agricultural exemption is to make your property a native species habitat. It takes little effort to provide what birds, snakes, ducks, coyotes and other creatures need to survive, i.e., food, water and shelter. Why not do this with the fifty acres, then leave this little strip of green to the city when I die? They can turn it into a park where people can go to rest, relax, walk and gaze at wildlife. As fast as green space is disappearing from the Dallas/Fort Worth Metroplex, it might be the only verdant strip of land left in a hundred years.

It sounds strange to relate, but that concept completely changed my idea about dying, and reversed the fear I had always felt. For some reason, leaving a wonderful piece of green that would provide protected habitat for animals as well as peace and serenity and a chance to be close to nature for people, gave my life (and death) new meaning. I could face not being around anymore if I knew I was leaving something worthwhile behind. My acceptance of death was complete when I made this decision.

Perhaps you have children and are proud of the way you raised them. You trust them to carry on a legacy of kindness and love. Maybe there is a cause that you really care about and you've provided for it in your will. Perhaps you have created something—art, poetry, movies, books—that made a difference, and you're leaving a piece of yourself that way.

The point is, that when I leave this earth, regardless of what is beyond it, I've left something wonderful behind. And that makes me very happy.

6. When You Look Good, You Feel Good

O r is it: When you feel good, you look good? I suppose an argument could be made either way. Regardless, being healthy and disease free is desirable whether you're thirty or sixty. And it's also number two on the "What Would It Take to Make Me Happy?" list.

Banish "All or Nothing" Thinking

Different people take different approaches to their health and well-being. Some say, "I'm happy the way I am—fat and all—and I don't want to do anything about it." Others say, "I need to lose twenty pounds, and I won't be happy until I do."

Both of these constitute "all or nothing" thinking, and are detrimental to your progress. The first one represents the fear of change that we talked about earlier. The second response reflects someone who is putting her life on hold until a certain event, which may or may not occur, happens. In which category do you fall? Or are you in a category all your own?

I was the latter and had put my life on hold because I wasn't perfect. A long laundry list of things I needed to do and accomplish before I started dating became my excuse for not embracing life, not looking for that special someone. They were: lose thirty pounds, have liposuction, get a facelift, get Botox injections, have my varicose veins stripped, have laser skin resurfacing. When I added up how much money it would take to get all these things (and more) corrected, it came to a hefty $50,000.

A good approach to either of these dilemmas is to create a goal that's only slightly more perfect than we are right now (after accepting ourselves as we are first). Make it a goal that's reachable within a foreseeable future. For example, I want to lose five pounds in two weeks, and once I've accomplished that, I will reward myself by going to the dermatologist and having the spider veins on my legs zapped. Now we have a win-win situation, and I am all the better for it and haven't spent $50,000.

The point is not to focus on the end result. It's better to strive to be healthy than to be thin. Reward yourself when you reach for good health and well-being. Give yourself an "'atta girl!" every time you eat your broccoli. Congratulate yourself many times during the day, give yourself some positive self-talk. Don't let other's negative attitudes slough off onto you.

When I tell people I want to live to be 150, most of them say they have no desire to live that long. They think one hundred is way too old. This usually comes from people under forty.

Attitude Key to Long Life

These days, living to one hundred isn't that difficult. People who live that long have several things in common. First, they are flexible. I'm not talking about their ability to do yoga or acrobatics. I'm talking about their attitude. They are able to take what they have learned in the past and apply it to new situations and experiences. They've discarded traditional thoughts and attitudes toward aging, and don't allow age to prevent them for engaging in any activities or interactions they desire. They don't think they're too old to have an active sex life, or run a marathon, or dance until dawn.

They seem to be able to use relaxation tools to overcome stress and anxiety. They meditate, or walk or relax in a chair without having to do anything, like read or watch TV. But most of all, and I have this in spades, *they want to live*. They are still excited about life. They eat well, exercise and participate in all kinds of mind-stretching and body-honing activities. They never stop learning new things, and they never tell themselves they're too old.

Our mental attitude makes all the difference. Some people are born old. Instead of growing up, they just get older. For these people, I would suggest regression. Think back to your childhood and remember how it felt to be young and uninhibited. Fantasize about running and playing with total abandon. Quit thinking that the whole word is watching you and judging you. The world is too wrapped up in its own problems to care much what you're doing. Let go of whatever's restraining you from being happy and doing the things you want to do.

Take Responsibility for Your Own Health

The best piece of advice I can give any Baby Boomer is to take responsibility for your own health. Slavish obedience to the American medical system will get you to the same place the rest of the aging population is at—sick, tired, old, and chocked so full of medications, they are barely conscious. Even most mainstream medical doctors admit 90% of what is wrong with Americans could be fixed or avoided by lifestyle changes. This country spends more money on health care than any other nation in the world, and yet we live shorter lives than most other developed countries.

I use the term "health care" with tongue in cheek. Doctors, hospitals, medical procedures and medications are not health care; they are "sick care." If you're healthy, you don't need the medical system. We spend more on sick care than all of our food, education and military spending combined. I think this reliance on the medical system is the principal reason. We know what we should be doing, we just don't want to. It's easier to take a pill.

Unfortunately, pills don't work. They may temporarily relieve a symptom, but they don't solve the problem. Here's an example. A doctor tells his patient he needs coronary bypass surgery. The patient reads Dr. Dean Ornish's book about reversing heart disease, abides by Dr. Ornish's plan (low-fat, vegetarian diet, exercise, and stress relief techniques), and essentially eliminates his need for surgery. Wouldn't you think his doctor would be elated? Wouldn't you think his doctor would spread the word to his other patients? Wrong! This information has been available to physicians and the general public for years, and yet I've never heard of a coronary bypass patient being given this option by his or her doctor. In fact, I've known several people who had bypass surgery, and their doctors never even told them to change their lifestyle one bit!

What am I saying? That our physicians don't have our best interests at heart? That they have their own agenda, and to hell with their patients?

Probably not. I'm just saying doctors are human, with all the frailties humans possess, and they grossly underestimate another human being's ability to make major lifestyle changes. Most of them don't tell us about options other than surgery because they've decided we wouldn't do it anyway. They are probably right, but shouldn't that be a decision the patient makes on her own after weighing all the options? Shouldn't doctors let us make our own decisions about what measures we are, or are not, willing to take to save our lives? I'm not accusing them of being inhuman, just short-sighted, tunnel-visioned conformists. In other words, human beings, just like the rest of us.

I only go to a doctor about every five to ten years. I'm not telling you to do that, but most people die in hospitals. Ever notice that? I try to stay away from doctors and hospitals. However, I recently decided my once-a-decade checkup was in order. I went to a young doctor, hoping against hope she might be more progressive, and not be trapped in the standard American physician mold.

I told her how old I was. The first words out of her mouth were, perhaps I should consider hormone replacement therapy. I told her that was totally unnecessary, as I had skated through menopause with no symptoms whatsoever, due mostly to my vegetarian diet and consumption of soy products. And anyway, didn't HRT cause breast cancer?

Even though it has been linked with breast cancer, combined HRT (estrogen plus progestin) nevertheless is prescribed to protect against osteoporosis, memory loss and menopausal symptoms. (None of which symptoms you would have had if you had followed a healthy diet, eaten soy products, and performed weight bearing exercise on a regular basis.)

Even when a landmark study linked HRT to heart disease and stroke in addition to breast cancer, the advice remained to consult one's doctor and weigh those risks against the alleged benefits mentioned above. Now, however, further research questions whether it ever had any affect on thinking impairment, except an undesirable one. In fact, three studies from the Women's Health Initiative have linked HRT with a higher risk of Alzheimer and dementia in older women. The very symptoms it was initially reported to help.

Further, HRT increases the risk of ischemic stroke, the most common type, by 44%. Incredible! Stay away from this stuff, and alleviate your symptoms using natural substances.

Natural alternatives to HRT are black cohosh, ginseng, licorice root and soy products. As a side-note, Premarin, which is short for "pregnant mare urine" (disgusting), is cruelly obtained from pregnant horses, and should be avoided for this reason as well as all the others.

My doctor still insisted it was warranted in some cases, but conceded that perhaps it wasn't necessary in mine. The next thing she suggested, since I had a history of alcoholism (I've been sober twenty years without the help of any kind of drugs), I might need to be on some type of antidepressant, like Zoloft, Prozac or Paxil. I said, "Why would I need to be on some drug that merely masks the symptoms, and won't allow me to discover the cause of my depression, if indeed I am depressed, which I'm not?" She conceded that point also.

She wanted to do a pap smear and a mammogram. I refused the mammogram. Haven't medical researchers tortured enough rats to figure out that radiation causes cancer? And aren't mammograms radiation? Hadn't she read the most recent information about mammograms which stated that they appear to be insignificant in detecting lumps early enough to make any real difference?

She gave up on the mammogram, and asked me to make a compromise. Would I let her do a pap smear this time, and the next time we could renegotiate? I allowed the pap smear. Who says I don't have the ability to compromise?

Am I telling you not to go to your doctor? Absolutely not! I'm merely telling you to take informed responsibility for your own health. You know your body better than any physician. And all medications have side effects, some of them potentially fatal.

Let's assume you don't want to live to be a 150 like me. Maybe you don't even want to live to be a hundred. I don't understand this, but maybe you are not having as good a time as I am. You don't want to give up all the good, fun things in life just so you'll live a few years longer.

Okay, I'll accept that. But forget about living longer. What about being crippled with arthritis, suffering penile dysfunction (primarily caused by prescription medications, illnesses such as diabetes or hypertension, or alcohol abuse), chronic pain, incontinence, and low or nonexistent libido?

Men Die First

The sad thing is that it is usually the men who die first. Their women spend a huge part of their later years taking care of an ailing man who most likely brought his problems on himself because of his stubbornness and refusal to modify his lifestyle. These women, who were the primary caretakers of children in their youths, are regressed back to babysitting, only this time it's their sickly husbands. They are deprived not only of their equal companions, but of the physical relations they are craving from their loved one. They're probably also dealing with ailing parents as well as their own health problems.

When you love someone, you want to take care of them. But my point is that much of this could be avoided, that both partners could be healthy, sexually active and vigorous throughout the last half of their lives. Making a few changes would be all that was required. Changes which, unfortunately, women seem more willing to make than men.

Women Choose Not to Remarry

I used to wonder why widowed and divorced women in their forties, fifties and beyond didn't remarry. I thought it was because men refused to marry older women when they could get younger ones. As it turns out, about 75% of the marriage breakups were initiated by women, with the end result that they cope better than the men they divorced. Women become highly self-sufficient. They achieve things that would have been impossible while they were married. They flourish on their own. The majority of them choose not to get into a new relationship.

Women don't want to get married again, especially not to men their own age. They are finally free, free to go wherever they want, pursue their own interests, and live mobile lives without the burden of a sick person who needs their constant nursing attention.

Men marry because marriage is most beneficial to them. They are taken care of. When women divorce them, they are at loose ends, are dismayed and cannot understand what went wrong. Many of them throw themselves into their work. Many immediately seek another relationship. Others are helplessly waiting until another woman comes along and wants them.

I know many men who really care about themselves and their bodies, who eat healthfully and exercise regularly. But they're the exceptions. It's not macho to eat fruits and vegetables. Red meat and beer are glorified as manly. His grill is man's best friend. The thing that makes a man "manly" (according to his own self-assessment) is his sexual prowess, and that's the very function he loses when he doesn't live a healthy life.

Think about it, boys. Don't do it to yourself or to your significant other. Dedicate yourself now to a healthy lifestyle. When your macho friends, with oxygen tubes dangling from their noses, are being pushed around in wheelchairs by their frustrated wives, you and your significant other will be engaging in long bouts of energetic lovemaking. That's about as macho as you can get!

7. Think Green

Now that we've got our Baby Boomer Bachelorette's head screwed on properly, let's move out of her head and into her body. Let's take a look at what's going on there. We can see fatty deposits around her thighs, stomach, waist and hips. Nothing unusual about that. She's well over forty years old and works in front of a computer all day. What did you expect? Too much fat, but her vital organs are looking pretty good. No major diseases detected there.

Excess fat's okay for an average working girl, but she's going to be in a major production. Is it possible to work some of that fat off her before she puts her ego out there in the competitive dating world? She has neither the time nor the money for liposuction.

First, let's check out her kitchen. Lots of vegetables, both fresh and frozen. Fresh and canned fruit. Soy milk. Excellent!

Is it necessary to belabor the health benefits of fruits, vegetables, whole grains, nuts and seeds? Is there an individual in the United States who has missed this news? Unfortunately, with the incomprehensible popularity of the Atkins diet, Americans are eating more meat and diary. We'll be seeing the results of this unfortunate trend in about ten years—more heart disease, diabetes, impotence, hypertension, etc.

Self-Destructive Fun

Why do our friends make it sound like more fun to eat something bad than to eat something good? I attended a very strict religious college, and we were always trying to put one over on the dorm mother. We tried every trick we could think of to slip past her without her noticing we had been drinking. That's childish behavior that is also self-destructive, but for some reason self-destruction seems to be "fun." I don't want to sound like an old fuddy-duddy. I believe in having fun, too. But it's not necessary to participate in things that are killing us in order to have a great time. I've had more fun since I quit drinking than I ever had when I was drinking.

A C-SPAN program showed another example of this self-destructive behavior. I'm a writer so I sometimes watch their book events. I'm not the only one, am I? A panel discussion featured four southern writers, two from Louisiana. These two began to discuss food, how it would be impossible for them to give up sausage gravy. It was their contention that if a food wasn't deep fried, it wasn't worth eating. These were southern traditions that went back to their ancient ancestors, and who were they to buck them?

The man and woman who were having this discussion were grossly obese, with bad complexions and sickly pallors.

Anyone watching this would have vowed to stay away from deep fried foods and sausage gravy just to keep from looking like these two.

Supplements

I do some supplementing, even though Tony Robbins calls vitamins "expensive urine." I'm not an authority on them, and can't really tell one way or the other if they are helping. I do know that I've dieted most of my life, and still restrict what I eat, so the supplements are a sort of "just in case" strategy.

Refined Sugar

I discovered some nasty information about refined sugar. According to my source, it is the worst enemy in our fight against aging. It increases the production of cortisol, an age-inducing hormone.

A diet rich in fiber (fruits and veggies—my mantra), nuts and soy products can lower bad artery-clogging cholesterol as effectively as medications. In a four-week study of forty-six adults, the LDL levels of those placed on a special diet that included almonds, grains and vegetables were reduced as much has those taking cholesterol-lowering statin drugs.

Begin to think GREEN. Kermit the Frog says, "It's not easy being green," but the very least I expect from you is to put more fruits and vegetables on your plate. Reduce portions of the high-fat, cholesterol-laden foods you now eat, thereby making more room for the green stuff.

Organic is good. Fresh is always best. The less processed the better, and eat less of it! Those are the standards by which you should judge your diet. Think Green!

8. Pain and Exercise Are Not Synonymous

Remember when Jane Fonda told us to "make it burn"? Do you recall, "No pain, no gain"? No wonder people don't want to exercise. Those machines at the health club look like the torture devices used on prisoners in the Tower of London. It seems obvious that the only way we're going to get in shape is to spend huge chunks of time hurting ourselves until we look like female body builders who look exactly like men except they don't have penises . . . I don't think.

It depends. If you want to look like a penisless man, you would have to be endowed with an overabundance of testosterone, or you could take steroids and pump up. But you can still lift weights and never come close to looking like a body builder. It'll just hone and tone your muscles, and you'll look smaller, even if you still weigh the same thing you weigh now.

Building Muscle is Desirable

Everybody knows muscle weighs more than fat, even though it takes up less space. How much you weigh could be irrelevant if you have enough muscle. Don't go out and buy expensive equipment you have no room for. You'll probably never use it once you take it out of the package, put it together and make yourself sore by overdoing it. If you like to exercise at home, there are plenty of exercises you can do with free weights. They don't require any special equipment other than a few various-sized weights that can be stored under your bed or in a wire rack in your closet.

How much time and effort you put into exercise will determine how your body will look. That's true of anything you do, so I'm not going to tell you that you can lift weights three times a week for thirty minutes and end up looking like Demi Moore in *Charlie's Angels*. However, you can be *healthy* with that kind of schedule, (if you include thirty minutes of vigorous walking three to four times per week, as well).

It's never simple, is it? Unfortunately, in order to be healthy, you must perform the acts required to create a healthy body. You already know what they are. You're just not doing them. Baby Boomer women are less likely to exercise than Baby Boomer men. Older boomers are more likely to exercise than younger boomers, but only 14% of all boomers exercise four to five times a week.

Too Little Muscle

We should be more worried about having too little muscle than too much. If we don't exercise, we lose five to seven pounds of muscle tissue every decade. This can create a couple of serious problems. The less you exercise the less you are able to exercise. You can't do as much as you used to be able to do. Your metabolism slows down and you use fewer calories. That creates more weight because you usually don't slow down your eating.

We've let our muscles go lax, and the fat and loose skin behind our arms is swinging like a hammock in the summer breeze. It's too late. We're too old to build muscle, and we might as well go ahead and give up, never exercise again, get sick and die. Right?

Older People Benefit Most from Weight Training

Wrong! A group of men and women participated in a two-month fitness program. Using machines, they performed strength-training exercises for 30 minutes two to three days per week. Surprisingly, the 61-80 age group gained a little more muscle in the same period of time than the 21-40 or 41-60 age groups (2.4 pounds as opposed to 2.3 for the younger group). Proof positive you can be any age and still gain muscle mass.

Self-Evaluation

Take a few minutes and do a self-evaluation. How flexible are you? Try touching your toes without bending your knees. Can you still squat without your knees creaking? Try climbing the stairs between two floors at your office. Can you do more than two flights without breathing heavily? Do you stand tall and walk with a springy step? Can you crawl onto the floor and play with your grandchildren? How much fat can you pinch around your waist? How's your posture? Are you getting that unsightly widow's hump?

Quality Time in the Gym Equals Quality Time in the Bedroom

Couples who exercise regularly reported having sex more often than nonexercising couples in their age group. In fact, couples in their sixties who exercised had sex more often than their nonexercising counterparts in their forties. Imagine spending more time in the gym contributing to more quality time in the bedroom.

If you presently have a significant other (and you will after you finish this book), exercise together. Evelyn, a 50-year-old with a taut body and a beautiful head of white hair, told me how sensual it was for her and her boyfriend (she met him through an Internet dating website) to work out together at the gym. Can't you just see your partner pumping the chest press while his pectoral muscles swell beneath his T-shirt? Guys, can't you see your girlfriend's thighs open and close as she works the adductor machine? Is it getting hot in here? The other good thing about having a partner is that you're more likely to work out with a friend encouraging you, and vice versa.

We've discussed menopause and HRT. One of the things prominently seen as a result of aging, especially in women, is osteoporosis. This debilitating disease is caused by the loss of bone proteins and minerals, which regular strength training can help prevent. Strength training can also improve your digestive system. It speeds up the process of moving food through your gastrointestinal system. If food stayed in there too long, you could develop cancer.

Something to note here, also. Since human beings have such long intestinal tracts, it naturally takes longer for us to digest food. It takes longer to digest meat than any other food, which may be one reason why the consumption of meat has been linked to cancer. Fruits and vegetables, on the other hand, run through your digestive system quite quickly—some fruits take as little as ten to twenty minutes to digest.

Why am I recommending strength training as opposed to aerobics? I'm not. I highly recommend aerobics—walking, running, bicycling, walking on the treadmill. But nothing will change the shape of your body faster than lifting weights. It is also possible to get an aerobic workout by lifting weights if you decrease the recovery time between machines or sets (a series of repetitions of one exercise) if you're using free weights.

Let's get our bachelorette started. She's pretty weak from not having moved her butt out of her rocking chair in front of the TV for quite some time. We'll have to start her off slowly. The first concern is safety. We need to lift the appropriate amount of weight that offers the proper amount of resistance without straining. The rule of thumb is to be able to complete eight to twelve repetitions, using a complete range of motion, with good form and without discomfort. Your muscle should be exhausted by the completion of the twelfth repetition. Increase your weights when you are able to do more.

Proper Form and Technique

Proper form is very important. You need to buy a book and read the instructions carefully, duplicating the exercise exactly as instructed. A better course is to go to a gym and have an instructor help you, or you could hire a personal trainer—an expensive route which only the more well-off can handle. If you've got an ex, and kids in college and a big house and car payment like most Baby Boomers, stick with the cheap YMCA membership or do it at home with free weights and an instructional book.

Lift the weights slowly and uniformly. Your greatest risk of injury is on the lowering movement, because that's when gravity tries to take over. Don't let it. Try two seconds for lifting and four seconds for lowering.

There's also another method that is excellent for increasing your strength rapidly. Try taking ten seconds to raise the weight and ten seconds to lower it. Doesn't sound like a long time, does it? Try it. It's an agonizing eternity, but it gets those muscles pumping. You might try this trick later, when you're a little stronger.

Be sure to warm up five or ten minutes before your exercise session and after. Run in place or treadmill before, stretch after.

Once again, I recommend books to help you with all of this. There is a list of recommended reading at the end of this book which will give you the names of several excellent books for weight training and exercising in general, whether you're a beginner or advanced. Joyce L. Vedral, Ph.D., an amazing woman in her late fifties, shows how weight training can transform your body at any age. I highly recommend all of her books.

If you're very, very weak, go to a gym or the YMCA and use strength training machines. Machines give you more control over the exercise, and you are in less danger of dropping too-heavy weights. In addition, there's always somebody there to assist you. Strength training using machines is great for the really lazy among us, because you get to sit down and exercise for most of the resistance machines. They restrict movement and isolate the target muscles, and even if you happen to drop the weight, it won't land on your foot. Even better, you don't even have to pick the weight up yourself. The Y would be good if you don't like to read books or learn new things on your own. They offer professional help at a reasonable price.

Weight training at home can save you money. All you really need are some progressively heavier weights as you get stronger, either barbells or dumbbells. Dumbbells take up less space because they don't have those long bars. When you tell people you work out with dumbbells, please make sure they know you're not talking about the relative intelligence of your exercise companions.

Consistency More Important Than Frequency

Consistency is important in strength training. Train your upper body one day and your lower body the next. Never train the same muscle two days in a row. Consistency is more important than frequency. A minimum of three days a week is recommended. A study showed that the difference between training three days a week and two days a week was minuscule, but only two days a week won't change your body very much.

In the best of all possible worlds, a four-day-a-week workout would be great, using the split system, i.e. training the upper body on even days, and the lower body on odd days.

Maybe every day for you is an odd day, but you know what I mean. If you employ the four-day-a-week method, you would be training every muscle twice a week. You should be seeing some significant differences in the way you look, assuming you are lifting heavier weights as you become stronger. There's another method called progressive resistance that is more complicated and takes longer. You can do that later, reading about it on my list of recommended books, if you really get into this weight lifting thing.

Well-Rounded Exercise

In order to make your workouts most effective in maintaining a youthful appearance and feeling like you're a youngster, it needs to be well-rounded. We have done strength training for our muscles, cardiovascular training for our hearts, but we need to add one other element to this. Flexibility training for our joints. Any good book about exercise will show you how to do stretching exercises. Often, they are done before and after you've participated in aerobics or weight-lifting.

Curves

The *Curves* system of exercising employs weight training in conjunction with aerobics. At their gyms, they place eight or ten machines, powered by hydraulics, in a circle, with "recovery squares" in between each machine. The beauty of these machines is that you work opposing muscles at the same time. For example, when you pull up, you work the biceps, and when you push down, you work the triceps, all on one machine. The faster you work the machine, the harder it becomes.

Meanwhile, a prerecorded tape tells you to "change stations," and you move to a recovery square. There, you jog or walk in place while maintaining your heart rate. After thirty seconds, it is time to change stations again. You move to the next machine, which might work your quadriceps as you raise the weights, and the hamstrings as you lower them. Once you have completed the circuit three times, you are asked to cool down using twelve stretching movements.

Do this a minimum of three times per week, although you could do more if you wanted. I recommend this method if the standard form of weight training is too time consuming for your schedule.

Our Baby Boomer Bachelorette has overcome her anxiety, she is eating right, building muscle, and burning fat. She is on the road to Boomer success, headed for a big payoff when her program is launched. We want to make sure she's at the top of her game. Is she ready for the big premier of her show, or is there something else that needs to be addressed first?

9. No Blue Bubbles

Consider what a new outfit can do for you. It can perk you up when you're down; it can give you the confidence you didn't have before; it can make you feel like a new woman. True, this may be temporary. But if you're feeling good about yourself after going through all the things we've put our Bachelorette through, then you're only going to need a temporary booster. You're feeling good on the inside; you're shaping up on the outside. Let's show the world you're proud of your accomplishments and happy to be a woman!

Semi-Extreme Makeover

Now is the time to call in the "makeup artist," the "hair dresser" and the "wardrobe person" to reinvent our star. If you can't make yourself over with the help of books and friends, then have a professional do it for you.

Do not rat your hair up into a bubble and spray it stiff, especially if it's dyed a silvery blue. It looks like a Dallas Cowboys' football helmet. People will be calling you "helmet-head" behind your back. Get a trendy 'do, or at least a classic one, i.e., a blunt cut or bob. Don't wear last decade's clothes. Go to a quality store and buy fashionable outfits. Try designer outlets and off-price shopping.

I don't expect you to wear low-slung jeans that reveal your navel, or belly shirts that ride up your midriff. I do expect you to wear those adorable capri pants with tops that don't look like oversized T-shirts. Don't pull extra-large T-shirts down over your hips in a feeble attempt to hide the fact that they've spread into the next county. If you're overweight, you cannot hide it. I didn't read that in a book. I've been overweight myself. If you know it, trust me, so does everyone else. Wear clothes that fit, not camouflage fatigues or sweats.

Heredity versus Environment

Research done on successful aging indicates that 70% of the characteristics attributed to aging are due to lifestyle choices. That leaves a mere 30% to heredity. You can't use the way your mother looked as an excuse. Even if your father ended up in a nursing home at seventy, it doesn't mean you have to end up the same way. Actually, only 4% of the population over sixty-five ends up in a nursing home, hospital or retirement facility. That's hardly enough to be considered unavoidable. That means the rest of us are free to age as healthfully, actively and attractively as we choose.

Avoid retirement communities like a cow patty in a pasture. It's like living in any community. When you are surrounded by a certain culture, mind set and example, you tend to adopt the same modes of behavior. In retirement communities, the talk is generally about so-and-so's latest ailments or the most recent death. You don't need that. Hang out with people who are young-thinking, vibrant and active. They're the ones to emulate, not the one's who have already given up.

In some places, however, the idea of a senior community is changing. Madeline Hill created a new concept in Ashland, Oregon. When she began wondering what the ideal senior community might be like, she came up with several principles upon which she was guided. It should not look like a senior community. It needed to be a part of the town in which it was located rather than set apart. The residents should be able to participate in the community life of the city, but have a rich community life at the residences. The community she built has sixty-five homes and one-hundred-sixty condominiums, all built in the early 20th Century Craftsman style. Her concept of "aging-in-place" sought to help seniors remain at home and independent while providing additional care when necessary (meals-on-wheels, home nursing, etc.). The idea was to live in your own home while still being part of a supportive community.

American Standard of Beauty

The American standard of beauty for women is exacting and unattainable. It's based on the images we see on TV and the movies, and no mortal woman can begin to live up to those images. It's easier for men, because women are more forgiving of them than they are of themselves. We can let our men have beer bellies, balding pates and flabby muscles, but we can never forgive this in ourselves. Although few of us ever attain this ideal, we never stop beating ourselves up for having flaws. I'm not sure where this comes from. I really don't think our men are as judgmental about our bodies as we are. Perhaps I'm wrong, but I don't think they see the same things as flaws that we do.

The Hollywood standard has become even more demanding than it was twenty years ago. The average size of models has shrank from an average of eight to ten to an unbelievable two to four. That's not only absurd, it's patently unattractive. While the female population of Hollywood is starving itself into nonexistence, the average female American is getting larger. America's obesity epidemic is all over the news.

The Right Size

How can you tell when you're the right size?

You can't tell by your weight on the scales. Your height, body type and muscle-to-fat ratio all play a part in how much you weigh.

You can't tell by your dress size. Clothes sizes are non-standardized and vary by manufacturer.

You can't tell by looking in the mirror. There are too many variations between mirrors—fat mirrors, skinny mirrors. Did you know if you lean a mirror against a wall rather than hang it, your reflection will appear thinner?

You can't tell by photographs. They vary according to the camera, film, lighting, poses, lens length, and many other factors.

So how can you tell when you're the right size? The only way to tell is how you feel about yourself. And that's mostly in your head.

Older Women Dating Younger Men

Why is it okay for Michael Douglas to marry Katherine Zeta-Jones, but it's treated as an anomaly when forty-year-old Demi Moore attracts at twenty-five-year-old Ashton Kutcher? I believe Demi and Ashton should be the standard rather than the exception. A recent AARP survey—one of the most extensive ever conducted on the dating and sex lives of midlife singles—stated that almost a third of unmarried American women between the ages of forty and sixty are going out with younger men! An astounding number given the social and historical precedent against it.

Generally, men die earlier than women. If you want your husband to live even close to as long as you do, it would be better to marry one at least ten years younger.

Patricia, a forty-two-year-old woman who said that she looked and acted younger than her actual age, wrote asking a dating guru for advice. She wondered why the men in her age group preferred younger women and what she could do about it. The advice columnist told the woman that she should sell what people were buying. In other words, Patricia should be content to date men ten or more years older than her, because they were the ones who wanted her.

I consider this very bad advice. Of course, date men your age or older, if you find someone you like, but go for the younger ones too. They live longer, have fewer age-related sex problems, and relate well to older women. If men your age are looking for younger women, then you should be looking for younger men. Not only do I suggest not being content with men ten or more years older than you, but I suggest not being content unless they are ten or more years younger!

I said our biggest fear is fear of change. What do you think is an over-forty woman's number one stumbling block to having sex again? Being naked. We're so afraid our bodies won't look good enough, that we forgo the pleasant activity of sex. Beatrice refuses to make love with the light on. Paula uses concealer creams to hide her scars and spider veins. Amber will not take her clothes off during intercourse. Mostly, though, we just don't make love to anyone other than our Jacuzzi—oops, I didn't mean to let that slip.

If women over forty are most afraid of taking off their clothes, what is an over-forty man's biggest fear? That it might rain and he won't be able to play golf on the weekend? No. It's the inability to perform. One book I read about this stated that women would rather have a tender lover (by that, I assume they mean an older guy) instead of a young stud strutting his stuff. On what planet? Women want hot, passionate, frantic sex just as much as men do. What the author of that book probably meant was that women prefer a kind, loving, tender man to a green kid who goes too fast and hasn't learned how to please a woman. However, I'd volunteer to help him learn. Wouldn't you?

Try not to idealize youthful sex as you experienced it. Think back. It really wasn't that great, was it? Another one of those statements I read in a book I'm still pondering. I'm thinking I should agree with it, but don't really. Anyway, think about what makes you a better person now: your inner beauty, kindness, generosity, pride in accomplishments—all the things you've become by virtue of living the number of years you have. These things translate themselves into an accomplished, companionable and exciting bed partner for any man, whether young or old or in between.

There are things you can do to maintain a youthful glow. We've already talked about diet and exercise, the two most important ones in the physical arena. We've talked about attitude, the number one element that keeps us young and vibrant.

But there are other things we can do to maintain our poise and grace. If anyone tells you something you feel, or think, or want to do, is inappropriate for your age, ignore them. Or even better, tell them to get a life. Never let someone else's negative self-image rub off on you. Don't dress like an old lady or an old man. Classic is best, if you don't already have a style. Shabby chic is not a style!

It's okay to fix some things about yourself that are fixable, and you can afford it. I'm an advocate of cosmetic surgery. Remember, however, that no matter how many face lifts, butt lifts, breast lifts and tummy tucks you have, it's all going to eventually fall again. There has to come a time in our lives when we can look in the mirror and accept the way we are at that moment. We must learn to find ways of feeling good about ourselves that aren't appearance-based. We can learn to accept our flaws and become comfortable with our bodies. The bottom line is, they are our bodies, we own them, and we must make friends with them.

List of Accomplishments

List the things you accomplished in the past decade, five years, one year, today. Did you have a meaningful conversation with your kids or grandkids? Did you take your dog for a walk and commune with nature? Did you write a letter to your elderly aunt who won't be around much longer? Did you write a few paragraphs on the memoir you've always wanted to write?

Did you read *Pride and Prejudice* again like I do once a year? What about any special abilities or talents you have? Did you use them today? Did you make a new friend or get in touch with an old one?

Is there something about your life you'd like to change? Make a list and start with the easiest one and work up. List each step you are going to take to change the thing you don't like. Is there something about your life you like? Enhance and magnify it, making a list of the steps you're going to take to achieve that.

How big of a change do you really want to make? We've written on our "What Would It Take to Make Me Happy?" list that we want to do something we love doing. I love lists!

I had never written a novel before. I read every book about writing and publishing I could find, joined an Internet writing workshop, joined a local writer's group, and took a novel writing course. My novel is presently being read by a well-known agency to see if they would be willing to represent me and my novel. Even getting your novel read by an agent is a major accomplishment. Getting an agency to take you on is like winning the Texas Lottery. Even if they don't take me, I'll keep trying and never give up. I'm not too old to accomplish anything I want, if I want it badly enough.

Doing Something You Love

If you are retired from the job you worked at for thirty years, you have an excellent opportunity to begin doing something you love doing, something that will give you purpose and keep you young. Baby Boomers have reached the age where they realize that their time on earth isn't forever, and that each moment counts. Many of us want to start living a different way, and making money doing something we love doing is our dream. Even if you're still working at your dull-as-dishwater nine-to-five (like I am), you can still formulate and put into effect a plan. That plan should enable you to change directions in a few years.

If you need to retrain, start while you still have your present job. Don't just quit Lame, Boring and Uninspiring, the law firm for which you presently work. Go about your change in an orderly, well-planned manner, and when you're ready, then quit. It's possible, if we retire early, to find ourselves in a financial position to take a lower-paying job that might be our dream job. We are able to rely on our financial reserves to fill in the gaps. Or work part-time in the field you're interested in. If you're retired, or in your spare time, begin a home-based business. I've done real estate investing and am now writing—the ultimate home-based business. It requires little overhead and virtually everything is tax deductible.

Rebel Against Middle-Age Expectations

Do something that goes against anything you've been told a so-called middle-aged woman is supposed to be able to do. I've got scuba diving and surfing on my list. What's on yours? Water skiing? Inline skating? Senior Olympics? Skydiving? Ballroom dancing? Snow skiing? Show all those people betting you can't do it that you can.

Douglas, an emotionally and socially backward man, had spent his entire life living close to his family. After his father and mother died, both of whom he nursed when they were ill, he did a complete about face. He began long-distance running, and eventually ran the Boston Marathon. That didn't satisfy Douglas, though. He went to Alaska and climbed Mt.

McKinley as a prelude to climbing Everest. When the political climate made going to Nepal impossible, he learned to ballroom dance. Given his reluctance to socialize, I found the ballroom dancing to be even more surprising than his Everest aspirations. People do change, often in drastic and amazing ways.

Do you surround yourself with supportive friends and family? We need people who believe in us to help us reach our goals. If anyone—and I mean anyone—is negative and tells you that you should "act your age," dump them. Don't ever let such a remark go unchallenged.

Our happiness list emphasizes the importance of friends and family, and this need cannot be overstated. Unfortunately, I don't have very many living relatives, and the few I do have live too far away for me to visit on a regular basis. I feel sad sometimes, but I have a network of close, dear friends, upon whom I rely for support, and with whom I feel connected. We meet for dinner, have parties at each other's homes, and go to the movies on weekends. We go out of our way to keep in touch, because it's so easy to become lax and allow relationships to lapse.

Nurturing

Nurturing and being nurtured are so important, we need some every day. If you have no family living with you, find nurture in other ways. That's why I have companion animals—one of the reasons anyway. I ALWAYS rescue them from the streets or adopt them from a shelter. I NEVER buy an animal from a backyard breeder or any kind of breeder. BILLIONS of unwanted dogs and cats—millions of them purebred—are being MURDERED in animal shelters every year. It's wasteful and ridiculous to buy them. Animals are not commodities or objects, like your living room sofa, to be bartered, bought and gotten rid of when it's no longer useful or appealing. When you adopt a stray, you win a heart forever, and will be rewarded in ways you'd never suspect. My dog and cat nurture me, give me unconditional love, and act like I'm the most wonderful person in the world. Boy, do I have them snowed!

We have to be happy in our independence before we can ever find someone with whom to be partnered. Our Baby Boomer Bachelorette says she's been happy many years being by herself, and we need to hurry this production up a bit so she can have some happy years being in a relationship. She's knocked off a few pounds, is glowing from her health-enhancing diet, and we revamped her sporty-natural style wardrobe with touches of the classic and the contemporary.

Her make-up is applied with a light touch. A sheer foundation and concealer is finished off with a natural powder to set it in place and make it last all day. A touch of neutral eye shadow, and her eyebrows are lightly penciled in, since, if you're like me, your already light eyebrows have faded even further. A nice powder blush to give her a glow and her eyelashes swabbed with some brown-black mascara to show how long and curly they are.

If she could have afforded it, she would have had liposuction on her tummy, thighs and hips, but that's not possible right now. She's saving toward that goal while continuing to pursue total health.

Beauty Tips for Women

Women, here are some basic beauty tips: eat right, exercise, stop smoking, stay out of the sun between the hours of 10:00 a.m. and 3:00 p.m. without sun block, and get plenty of sleep. Engage in a skin care ritual. Keep your makeup soft and natural. Wear flattering colors and—most of all—be happy. Nothing makes you more beautiful than inner beauty radiating on the outside. Get excited about life. It will show on your face.

According to a character in my favorite author, Lawrence Block's, novel *Small Town*, it's a mistake for women to knock themselves out trying to attract men. According to this character, all we have to do is be "available." Men don't care if we wear designer outfits, or if our shoes and purses match those outfits. These are the only things men are concerned about: "Did you have tits? Did you have an ass? Did you have a mouth? Did you have a pussy? Were any or all of these available to him?"

I can't help but believe there's some truth to that.

Beauty Tips for Men

Basic beauty tips for men: If you're going bald, don't grow the hair long on one side and comb it over to hide your bald spot. The Benny Hinn look is out. If you're balding, shave the whole thing and do the Vin Diesel look. He's hot. Want facial hair? The Foo looks great with a shaved head. If you can afford it, hair transplants are sometimes helpful. Do not, under any circumstances, wear those old-fashioned aviator style glasses frames. Small frames or frameless glasses are the new look. Adopt it. Eat right and exercise goes without saying. Smile and keep your wardrobe updated. It may look cool to your buddies, but a beer belly protruding from a Hawaiian shirt is not going to attract women, unless you happen to be rich and famous, in which case, anything goes.

Our Bachelorette is getting excited thinking about the male of the species, so let's get this show on the road.

10. What Do Women Want?

It's taken some time, but we've finally got our Baby Boomer Bachelorette to a place where she's at least willing to look for love. She's accomplished, or is on her way to accomplishing, all the steps on the happy list. She's developing a relationship with a higher power; she's working on her health and fitness; she's writing the Great American Novel, thereby doing something she loves doing; and she has close friends and family who support her in her endeavors.

The situation reminds me of a speaker I once heard. He was driving along, and a little dog started chasing his car down the street. The dog was running for all he was worth, using everything inside him to catch up with the moving vehicle. The driver abruptly stopped, opened the car door, and looked at the panting little dog. "Now what?" he asked.

Now What?

Good question. We've been moving so fast, we need to stop and take stock of where we are, what our goals are, and how we want to reach them. We need, in TV production lingo, to identify and analyze our "target audience." What kind of person do we want to attract? What is his or her age, socioeconomic status, education level? What kind of person do we want to make sure we don't end up with, i.e., some of the losers we've ended up with in the past? How are we going to present ourselves to prospective dates and/or mates to be sure we appeal to exactly the kind of person we want to attract? Is it love we're looking for, or something a little less committed?

In order to be successful, the production must in some way affect the audience emotionally. We need to define exactly what our hopes and expectations are. More importantly, we need to decide our "program content," that is, what we want to project.

We don't really need somebody to complete us. We could live the rest of our lives without finding a life's companion or, God forbid, without ever having sex again. My mother, whose husband (my father) died when she was thirty-five, never had another man until the day she died at the age of seventy-six. I'm determined not to end up like that. Even if I don't find my "soul mate," I still intend to have sex at least once more before I die. Don't you?

Why You Are Lovable

Instead of looking for someone to love, or to love you, look at all the reasons why you're lovable. List them, of course!

They're probably the same things that make you lovable to somebody else. Looking to another human being, whether male or female, for confirmation will always make you half a person. Hopefully, you're growing, and the person you choose to share your life with, whether it be for a short period or a long one, will be growing also. You can help each other grow and reach your mutual or individual goals.

One source I consulted stated that it upset him when women said men didn't show emotions. He stated that if the only emotion they are showing is happiness, it must mean that they are happy. Does that mean women only count unhappiness as an emotion? This is another one of those instances where I read something that sounds true, but might not necessarily be. No one is happy all the time, are they?

Perhaps now is the time to ask the question, "What do men want?" Shana, a young woman happily married for a number of years, supplied a simple answer. Although I wanted to dispute it, I really couldn't. She said, "There are only a few things that men want: a pretty wife, regular sex, enough money and a good-looking car." Whether you concur or not, I think we can all agree that men's needs appear to be simpler than women's. I've had men agree with this assessment, and I've had men disagree. Jerry said it was probably what most men wanted, but he put himself in a different category, a slightly elevated one. He thought she forgot about home and family, honesty and integrity, which were important to him. What do you think?

We're all human beings—not just black or white or protestant or catholic or liberal or conservative or whatever. We want to meet someone with whom we have things in common, but we also need to learn to appreciate what's unique in others. It could help expand our horizons.

Someone with similar values would enhance a relationship and keep it from being so much work. We're always hearing that old adage that you have to work at a relationship. I work all the time. I don't want to have to work at something that's supposed to be fun.

Edward, a long-time bachelor, finally married in his forties. He said one of the most eloquent things I've ever heard about marriage: "If I'd known it was going to be this easy, I'd have done it a long time ago." Now there's a happy, compatible marriage (assuming his wife feels the same way). If you're consistently compromising your personality and your beliefs to be with someone, then it's too much work.

I've always dated men who disapproved of me. These relationships never worked out because, instead of finding someone who was my equal or had the same or similar values, I always found men who were "less than" me. They were less educated, made less money, and had no real substance. In order to raise themselves up, they had to bring me down. It was an unhappy and uncomfortable situation all around.

Zoey has been married to the same man for twenty-five years. She described her relationship with her husband this way: "He's the only man I've ever been able to completely be myself around." In my youth, when I was with a man, I felt as if I had to act a certain way. I was afraid when he got to know the real me, he wouldn't like me. Low self-esteem, you'd say. But I think it goes deeper than that. I believe women are given a certain code of behavior and appropriateness that they feel they have to abide by. When they are unable to, because it conflicts with their basic nature and personality, they avoid, like myself, the situation that provokes these feelings.

Is Self-Esteem Necessary?

Which brings us to the question: Do you have to have self-esteem in order to get dates? Probably not, at least you don't have to be all the way there. I doubt if anyone else is either, although some may appear to be more confident than others.

Recent information regarding self-esteem indicates that it may not be the solution to all our problems like we've been led to believe. Apparently, many of us seem to be functioning just fine without much of it. Self-esteem fluctuates within the same person. It may be high one day or under one set of circumstances, but it may be low at another time. It is difficult to measure. While it's true that most successful people have it, there's no research to indicate that unsuccessful ones don't have it. The people who seem to have it in large quantities are criminals, cons, bullies and other nefarious characters.

The Self-Esteem Myth

Middle-aged women are particular prone to buy into the self-esteem myth. We've read too many books (I have, anyway) about why we are the way we are, and find ourselves attributing our failures in the romance area to childhood abuse, or an alcoholic father, or what I call the "abandonment syndrome." That's when a parent leaves us early in life either by death, desertion or divorce, and the rest of our lives are colored by this event. We've cast ourselves as victims of our circumstances, and have allowed our labels to dictate our lives.

Susan, who grew up with a denigrating mother and an absent father, appears to suffer from low self-esteem. She is nevertheless married to a man fourteen years her junior who loves and cherishes her. After many years of marriage, she still says she expects him to leave her any minute. She can't understand why he stays. She worries about looking older and being over-weight. It's obvious to her friends why he married her and continues to stay with her. She's a lively, companionable and loving person. She and her husband are compatible and love each other very much. Who's to say she isn't successful at romance?

We have very little if any control over our feelings. They are just that—feelings, and it is not necessary to act on them. Our thoughts are easier to control than our feelings, but our behavior is the easiest of all. I subscribe to the school of behavior modification. Take the action, and the thoughts and feelings will follow.

Men Looking for Women Their Age

According to one source I read—another one of those things you want to believe but don't quite—is that men over fifty are looking for women of the same age. I think we can safely exclude Hollywood men in this group, but we're talking about average, normal guys (ever met one of those?). There are lots of reasons why this might be true. Not everyone bases their relationships on looks. Besides, Baby Boomer Babes can be quite stunning. Most men in their forties and older really don't want to start another family. They've got the first ones out of college and aren't willing to put another bunch through. There are always exceptions to this, however.

Most of us want someone who can relate to our experiences in the sixties and seventies. Antonia told me she had dated a guy twenty years her junior. When she asked him where he was when Kennedy was shot, he said, "Nowhere. I wasn't born yet." That's some embarrassing pillow talk.

Romance, contrary to what we see on TV and at the movies, is not for the young, thin and beautiful. It's for us because we *are* young, thin and beautiful!

Game Playing

I've read a lot of profiles that say they don't want to play games and aren't interested in anyone who does. That baffled me at first. What games were they talking about? It then occurred to me that when we are young and had lots of eligible men, we believed that if we treated them cavalierly or made them jealous with other men, or pretended indifference, it would make us more desirable. Truly mature people are not interested in these types of games, and they are certainly not interested in creating the pain that is the result of them. Don't be one of these people.

Now, we've isolated our target market for the production. We want someone with similar values, but not so much like us that we can't benefit from our diversity. We want someone who is happy, but is able to show other emotions. We want someone approximately our own age, or in the case of women, a little younger, since we don't want him to die before we do. We want someone with similar interests, background, and financial status, but don't want to limit ourselves too much. We want someone who takes care of himself, but isn't priggish about it. Most of all, we want someone who is warm, loving and ready for a relationship.

What, then, don't we want?

11. Productions in the Past

We've identified our target audience, the people we want to watch our production and respond to it. The next step in the preproduction phase of the program "Baby Boomer Bachelorette—the Miniseries" is to check out similar productions in the past. If we're going to make mistakes on this new venture, we need to at least make new mistakes. How will our present production differ from the successful and unsuccessful efforts that we've made in the past?

Examine Past Relationships

Examine your past relationships, give them a good going over, and discover what about them you need to avoid in your future relationships.

Perhaps you're like me, a woman who loves too much. Remember that book? From what I remember about it, a woman who loved too much would find a man like her daddy—most likely a charming alcoholic type who had abandoned her—and try to make their relationship turn out differently. That is, he reforms and never leaves her. Usually, this situation is destined for failure because the woman, me, inevitably ends up being deserted. Unfortunately, she gets a major adrenaline rush out of the deal, and her depleted reserves must constantly be revitalized by finding another man just like the last one and going through the process all over again. Pretty soon, it's like beating a dead horse. The adrenaline just won't respond anymore, but she keeps repeating the pattern, always hoping.

My last long-term relationship happened about ten years ago. I thought he was the man of my dreams. We met in a twelve-step group, and it was instant adrenaline. He was tall and handsome and very personable. Everybody liked Jake. My advice: steer away from someone that EVERYBODY likes. Chances are they're a chameleon who changes to fit whatever company they're in at the time. The problem is that they have no real substance, and do not know who they are themselves.

In a long relationship, you eventually have to start being who you really are, and if you're a ghost, you're forced to move on. That's what Jake did, and not just with me. He had a pattern of bouncing from one woman to the next. His friend told me he lasted longer with me than anybody else, but it wasn't very long. There's a lot of pressure on a man who has to be what everybody wants him to be. When two people he is simultaneously trying to please come into conflict, which is what happened to Jake, he can't hold up, because he has no real position himself. He's torn between the warring factions, desperately trying to please them both, and not succeeding with either one.

After Jake dumped me, I spent the next ten years living with insecurity. If I had been twenty-five and had lost my boyfriend, I most likely would have gotten over it as soon as I began dating someone else. In my forties, after experiencing many painful losses (including divorce and death), being more mature and feeling more strongly about someone, it took me a long time to heal. I believed there must be something terribly wrong with me for him to leave me like that. It's taken a long time to realize there isn't anything wrong with me. Well, a couple of things, of course, but we've already successfully addressed them.

I hope to break my pattern by being more realistic in my dating. I want to hang out with people who are different than that, who have more stable backgrounds, and have their feet more firmly planted on *terra firma*. I'm going to have to keep a wary eye out to avoid being attracted by the same type of man again. As Tony Robbins says, "The past does not equal the future."

Who to Date

If I want to be around active people, or creative people, or people who cherish family connections, those are the type of people I must seek out. I want someone who will support me in my efforts to achieve my goals, one of which is to be a published author. Therefore, I might want to hang out with creative people—writers, artists, etc. I don't want to associate with people that are too esoteric, so I also need to seek out the active types, ones who like to participate in new activities.

Who not to date: people you work with. This can create a potentially uncomfortable situation in which one of you—usually the woman—is forced to move on. In this economic climate, the last thing you want is to lose your job.

Don't raise your expectations too high. You are meeting human beings, not movie stars. They are going to have the same hangups, issues and problems that you do.

Some say as we age, we become more set in our ways. I take issue with that notion. Are we really set in our ways? Being told that is insulting, as if we were too old and stupid to change, and it's patently untrue. We are in a unique position to be able to change. We have lived long enough to learn from our past mistakes. We've changed often enough, whether forced to or voluntarily, to know that, while it may be temporarily painful, it's ultimately worth it. Our experiences tell us the best way to accomplish the change.

Who else should we watch out for? Alcoholics, workaholics, dope fiends—all the types Bridget Jones was wary of? Not necessarily. Some of the best people in the world are recovering alcoholics. Note that I said *recovering*. Still, you're taking a chance on people with fatal flaws, but I guess we all have flaws, although most of them are not fatal.

Everybody Has Baggage

I've read in the personals that some people don't want anyone with "baggage." It was number one on both men and women's most undesirable traits in a potential date in the AARP survey.

My response to that: You must have been in a coma for the past forty years if you don't have any baggage. The trick is not to carry the excess around with you, and not let it drag you down. As far as completely getting rid of it—maybe on your death bed you won't have any hangups.

You won't, but I'll probably be in the process of overcoming yet another addictive behavior—whatever that might be. I'll have a small bag of regrets, addictive behaviors and longings clutched firmly to my dying chest, determined to carry them with me beyond the grave.

If your loving spouse of thirty years died of cancer, you'll have a special set of circumstances to overcome. A spouse who dies is usually held up as a standard for all future relationships to live up to, and that's always tough. Give yourself plenty of time to mourn. It sometimes takes years.

My mother and my sister were both widowed at an early age—my mother at thirty-five and my sister at twenty-five. My mother never found another man who could live up to my father's image, and I'm beginning to wonder if my sister ever will. It's difficult to find another man who's a saint when you have to live with him every day for the next fifty years, and you know all his secrets and idiosyncracies.

Analyze your past relationships, see where you went wrong, ask friends who have known you for a long time for help, and avoid making the same mistakes this time. If we keep doing the same things over and over, we're always going to get the same results. It's time to do something different.

Michael, a youthful-looking over-fifty Boomer, was married the first time for 20 years and the second time for 10 years. According to him, he's had two successful marriages. "You're only fifty-five," I told him. "You still have plenty of time for a couple more successful ones."

If your past productions were unsuccessful, make the necessary changes to ensure the success of the new one. If they were successful, then, by all means, continue to do what works. There's a lot riding on our series, and we want to make sure it's the best product we can make it.

12. A Sponsor Who Believes in the Product

L et's take one final look at our product—Baby Boomer Bachelorette. Is she everything she can be? Probably not. She's a work-in-progress, and will never be perfect. That's okay. We just need to find someone who values our product as she is. We want to make as sure as we can that we get a good return on our investment. The way we do that is to appeal to a "sponsor" who believes in our product. But where will we find him?

Meeting people of the opposite sex was easy when we were in our twenties and thirties. Everyone our age was single and looking for the same things we were—fun, sex and possibly romance. Aren't we still looking for the same things when we're in our forties, fifties and beyond? Wouldn't it be nice if the men we rejected in our youths would miraculously reappear, and we'd have a second chance at them?

I wish I could make Jim, the cool guy I threw over in college, unmarried and available. He's an airline pilot with whom I have a lot in common, and I dumped him for an alcoholic, pathological liar. We still occasionally see each other on a friendship basis. *Heavy sigh.*

Most everyone our age is married, and if the men aren't married, give it fifteen minutes, and they will be. A single Baby Boomer man is a prime target, and apt to be deluged with single females at or near his age. They don't remain single for long.

Baron, a pudgy fifty-something with a receding hairline, divorced after twenty years of marriage. It only took him one year to find another woman to marry. How did he meet her? They went to the same church, and she saw that he was in pain because of his divorce. She gave him a shoulder to cry on, and a kind and understanding person to talk to. It didn't take long for friendship to turn to romance, and they were married shortly thereafter.

The truth is, men benefit more from marriage than women do, and they love being in the marital state. That's not necessarily true for women. We need to decide if that's what we're looking for when we begin dating again. I'd wager a guess that's what most men are looking for, especially if they've had a happy or comfortable previous marriage.

Where Do We Meet Bachelors?

Since these available bachelors are scarce and quickly snatched up, where do we meet them? The first suggestion I usually receive is to meet them through friends. Ha! Ha! I only know one man over the age of forty who is single, and none of my friends whom I've asked know any. Or are they just saying that because they know me too well to introduce me to any of their friends? Whatever the reason, my friends haven't been forthcoming in the man department.

I read about sixteen single women over the age of forty who got together and threw a party. Each of them brought an eligible man that they didn't necessarily want to date, but who might appeal to someone else. Do I know sixteen single women? Easily. Do I know sixteen single women who know sixteen eligible men? No way! Most of the single women I asked didn't know ANY single men over forty. (Not any heterosexual ones, at least.)

Bars? Boring. Besides, there's nothing more pathetic than seeing the over-forty crowd in a smoke-filled nightclub, looking slightly droopy and insecure, seeking love. Leave the partying for the twenties and thirties crowd. The exception to this would be for those who like to dance.

Annabeth, a blonde with a spontaneous personality, met her husband at the airport. They were unable to get on a flight because they were both flying standby. She highly recommends this method of meeting men, but I'm afraid I'd be arrested if I hung out at D/FW Airport too often.

Hobbies, sports, church, activities? All excellent possibilities, but too hit-and-miss. You might want to run the Boston Marathon, but what realistically are the possibilities of meeting an eligible man while you're fighting to keep from fainting? Is it really possible to talk after running twenty-six miles?

I'm heavily into do-it-yourself home improvement and spend quite a bit of time at Home Depot. Would I like to meet a guy who's handy with tools? Boy, would I! But I rarely wear my ball gown to the home improvement center. I usually wear no makeup, a pair of tights that are either marked with paint or have bleached-out spots on them. They're topped of with a holey T-shirt that says, "Animals—It's Their World Too," or "What is Mr. Winkle?" I doubt if too many guys would be attracted to this attire even if the T-shirt said, "Show me *your* Mr. Winkle!"

I also joined a local writer's group—not necessarily to meet men, of course, but to make myself a better writer. If there happened to be an attractive, eligible man there, that would be okay. You probably won't believe this, but writers are kind of nerdy. Well, not all of them. *I'm* not nerdy, but many of us are. As per usual, the only attractive one was already married.

Darcy discovered the most original way to meet a man. She experienced the ultimate in the "cute meet." She met him in cadaver class. A massage therapist into some sort of energy healing type deal that I don't understand, she paid, along with several others, to dissect a used cadaver. It just so happened that she spotted the love of her life across the naked corpse. I wouldn't recommend rushing out to sign up for cadaver class, however. I'm betting this was a once-in-a-lifetime event and not easily duplicated, even if one might want to.

Cyber-Dating

I've pooh-poohed most of the usual ways of meeting men, but is the most important one not obvious? The one that is the most efficient, gets the quickest results, and gives you an opportunity to get to know something about the guy before you have to go on a date with him?

And what way is that? The modern way, the progressive way, the new millennium way. ONLINE! CYBER-DATING!

13. I've Fallen and I Can't Get Up

My first experience with meeting a man on the Internet was not through a date-seeking website. It was through an Internet workshop for writers. This workshop operates by allowing writers to submit their works to other writers for critique purposes. You, in turn, critique their work.

A raucous, in-your-face writer began subbing his novel about a raucous, in-your-face alcoholic, written in the vein of the Beat Generation authors. Even though shocked, I was instantly interested. We had a lot in common as recovering alkies, and we soon began a hot and witty correspondence outside the group.

After several months, I was on my way to his state to meet Scott (but not until I had his full name, address, telephone number and recent photograph). If he looked even half-way decent, I intended to be on my back faster than you could say,

"I've fallen and I can't get up!" Obviously, I hadn't had sex in awhile, and sure enough, he was good enough to get me on my back for the first time in two years.

Sad to say, however, it didn't work out. I never told him how old I was, and he never asked, never learning he was ten years my junior. I had sent him a recent photograph, but he never asked. Anyway, the age difference wasn't the problem. The problem was my inability to accept things for what they were without projecting them into something they could never be. I wanted someone who was financially stable, could afford to visit me in Texas and meet my friends, and encourage me in my aspirations of becoming a novelist. Scott looked down on my style of writing—too lightweight for Mr. I-Write-What-I-Want-No-Matter-Who-It-Offends-So-Fuck-Off.

Did this sour me on Internet dating? Not at all. It made me realize it was a fabulous source for singles, and that I merely needed to be more in control of who I decided to meet.

The midlife dating game was one that we older people could approach with practicality. It didn't have to be like when we were younger and tackled it with our adrenaline flowing and our hormones raging. We no longer had the attitude that a man must pursue us, while we perpetually teased and put him off, hoping his persistence would eventually win us over. We no longer believe that destiny controls our romantic lives. They could be controlled by us.

Internet Dating

America—the world, it seems—has a fascination with the Internet. I'm not quite sure why. Perhaps the enchantment of immediate access is too much for us. I have it at work, at home, and I'd probably have it in my car if I could. Almost anything we want to know about is on the Internet, and it's at our fingertips, free for the asking. Instant service, instant gratification.

It's only natural that we would begin to use the world wide web to find a date. It's so much easier to go online and look for love than risking that we might run into the love of our lives in a bar, restaurant or home improvement center.

Some people criticize Internet dating—usually smug married people—stating that it's unlikely one would find true love there. But, consider, what are the odds of finding someone any other way? We act as if we had it all planned out, and that meeting them in the airport or over a cadaver was perfectly natural, and not at all serendipitous. But we know that's not true. My premise is that we're just as likely to meet our match through an Internet dating service as we would playing volleyball at the beach or being introduced by friends. In a way, it's kind of the same as being introduced by friends. They've been prescreened, as our friends would do for us, but in this case we've gotten a look at them first.

Writing the Script

This brings us to the "script" stage of our production. We need to plan our presentation in all its aspects to give it a better chance of succeeding. We need a full-blown script in order to get our production under way.

The Profile. The profile is what we plan to say about ourselves on the dating service we choose in order to attract the largest number of responses. It also addresses what we are looking for in another person. It's better to emphasize our assets, however, rather than writing a detailed, meticulous profile of what we are looking for. It would be a mistake to be too narrow because we might miss out on some great people. The things to be specific about are characteristics you would consider intolerable in another person, like religion, age, or smoking.

Part of the script will also entail our photographs, consisting of several different poses and angles. One or both of these items could go through several changes and numerous revisions before we get it exactly like we want it. Some things to think about while composing these aspects of our "script" are: (1) audience appeal (who are we trying to attract and how best to do that), and (2) pace (what length should our profiles be, how many photos and what poses). Most importantly, what are the potential problems with either one that need to be ironed out before we actually air the program?

Of the millions of personal ads on the numerous websites, the over-fifty crowd accounts for somewhere between 11% and 50%, depending on the publication. Where else would you be able to expose yourself to so many eligible bachelors? Remember when your mother scolded you for "exposing" yourself in public. Forget your mother! Completely put everything she said about being demur out of your head. We're starting from a whole new perspective, one in which you want to expose yourself as much as possible to the greatest number of people possible.

The Photographs. Let's talk about our heroine's photos. Her chances of receiving more replies will increase if she puts a photo with her profile. Every website says that, and it's true. Even if you aren't that great looking, most people are going to want a photograph of you sooner or later. They're eventually going to meet you in person, so you might as well be up-front about your looks. If they're not going to like you because of the way you look, it's better to know about it before you spend the time and/or the money to meet them. People age so differently, and, let's face it, some just look much younger than others the same age. It's something we're going to have to deal with.

Our heroine's not the ugliest chick in the nest, but she's no Pamela Anderson either. It is possible to have a flattering photograph taken of yourself that will increase your chances of getting responses, but keep it casual. I think most of us respond to a relaxed photo rather than a formal one, unless you are using several photos, in which case definitely show yourself in your tuxedo as well as your dockers.

Tiffany, who has been doing this for years, says the more photographs, the better, and to unequivocally include a full-length one. You will be rewarded with even more responses. Of course, it might have had something to do with the fact that she lost sixty pounds after gastric bypass surgery. But, regardless of whether you've lost weight or not, it's better to be as up front as possible about the way you look.

Deanna told me about the three-hundred-fifty pound woman who sent a prospective date her picture. He lived in another state, and they communicated for a long time via e-mails. He eventually came to visit. What she hadn't told him was that the picture she sent him was several years old. She actually weighed three-hundred-fifty pounds, not one-hundred-fifty. The minute he deplaned and saw her, after giving her a screaming lecture in the terminal, he turned around and booked a flight back home. This is perfectly understandable, and you should never play this sort of trick on a man.

It is not impossible for an overweight person to find romance on the Internet. Zack, weighing in at two-hundred-fifty, did, and he's now married. I could name several other couples who experienced the same thing. Love's not just for the thin, just like it's not just for the young.

We base a lot on the way another person looks to decide whether to respond to them or not, and it's not necessarily if they're good looking. I've found myself being unwilling to respond to someone who appeared to be quite good looking, not because I don't think I deserve someone handsome, but because there was something about them that didn't appeal to me. I can't explain it. Maybe they remind me of an ex. If they're wearing a cowboy hat or holding a dead fish, you can bet I'm not going to respond.

Look your best, look happy, and make sure it's a recent shot that is clear and not grainy. Several shots would be ideal: one casual and smiling, one more formal and one full-length. One of you participating in a favorite activity, such as a marathon, hang gliding or skiing, would be great. Lose the sunglasses. Everybody looks glamourous in sunglasses, and they are not a true representation. Wear your most complimentary color and make sure the background is not distracting.

Some people recommend that you do not include your dog or cat in your photo, but I disagree with this. Since I'm an animal lover, I like people who care enough about their companion animals to include them in their pictures.

Help from the Camera Operator. We may need the help of a "camera operator." It might be a friend or it might be a professional. I'm a pretty good photographer, and took most of the pictures of a friend that she posted with her profile. If you have a friend like me, trade them something you're good at (like painting or yard work) for them taking your photo. If you're a female, make sure the photographer has a soft focus filter over the lens. If you don't have any friends who can take a quality photo, hire a professional. It'll be worth the money, and you can give prints to your relatives for special Christmas presents.

I would also advise against using a digital camera. While they are great for snapshots and family vacations, their resolution is still not high enough, the grain is not fine enough, to take a quality portrait. You'll look older and rougher than you really are. It's okay to scan an already existing photo, but make sure the resolution on your scanner is good.

Do not use a group photograph and do a bad job of cropping the other people out of it. There's nothing more irritating than a disembodied arm circling your neck, unless it's a group shot that has not been cropped, and the viewer doesn't have a clue which one is you. Have a photo taken especially for your profile and make sure it's a good one (or two or three).

Let me pause for a moment to scold those who have already placed a photograph along with their profile on a matchmaking website. I've seen some incredibly ugly, unflattering pictures of overweight women wearing bulky sweatshirts lying on the sofa with their hair sticking out from every angle. Shame on you! Unless you're trying to attract another lazy slug, who's primary interests are sitting in a recliner dressed in his jockey shorts and swizzling Budweiser while he watches Monday Night Football and ignores you, then do not put such photographs on the Internet for millions to see!

Have some pride. Show the best side of yourself that you possibly can. Don't skimp on the photographic aspect of your profile. Think what you want your photo to say about you. If you want the world to know you're a slouchy couch potato, then certainly keep the one of you watching TV on the sofa in your Texas A&M sweatshirt.

One last cautionary tale about photographs. Don't send people pictures that might offend them. It states specifically on my profile that I love animals of all types. When a man sent me photos of himself with his e-mail, one of them was of him standing over a dead tiger, or bobcat or some other type of big cat, with a gun on his shoulder. The message was obvious. He was a big game hunter. How could I possibly be interested in someone who wantonly murders animals? I sent him a return e-mail telling him that very thing. The next e-mail I received from him stated that the cat had killed several children in a South American village, and that's why he killed it. Was this supposed to make me feel better? First of all, I didn't believe it. Second, what was he doing in a primitive village where people were still being eaten by tigers? I ended the correspondence right there, although some people might have thought what he had done was heroic.

Don't send obscene pictures of your naked body, thereby proving how well-endowed you are. That's a definite no-no and will get you kicked off a cyber-dating website.

Now go to one of the dating websites and look at some of the ads so you'll get some ideas about what to do and what not to do, even though I'm going to tell you that in the next chapter.

14. The Script

You've now looked at quite a few profiles on the Internet dating services, and you may be feeling rather discouraged. When I first perused them, I felt as if I'd been abducted by aliens and had woken up on Planet "Stepford Singles." I'd never seen a greater collection of people whose lives were so well put together—no baggage, always happy, energetic, athletic, and the incredible number of senses of humor was amazing.

Here's Guy's self-description:

> *I'm a rare individual who's exceptionally diverse in his characteristics, talents and interests. An ivy league class act with roguish tendencies and a great sense of humor.*

I like his "class act with roguish tendencies." It shows he put some thought into it. No self-doubt from this one.

Here's another one:

*I'm a handsome, intelligent, successful, athletic,
All-American guy who loves to travel and
experience life and the world...*

Sounds perfect, doesn't he? Don't despair. He's just
doing what you're going to be doing, and that's letting us know
what his best qualities are. We'll have to wait until later to find
out the bad news. Nobody's going to telegraph their
idiosyncracies over the world wide web.

Don't stray so far from the truth that you're going to get
found out the minute you meet your potential dates. That's one
of the biggest complaints about Internet dating—the person
doesn't live up to their profile. I'm not talking about not
looking like your photograph. It should go without saying that
you must post a recent photo. If you say you run marathons, but
can't walk across the room without losing your breath, don't
make that claim. If you say you're cheerful and outgoing, but
are really a morose misogynist, do not sign your e-mails with
a happy face.

Allan told me the second person he e-mailed turned into
a two year relationship. When that one ended, so did his luck.
When he began dating again, his very first Internet date ended
up in the emergency room with a severe asthma attack. Allan
became frustrated with "fake profiles, fake photos, old photos
and glamour shots." More often, he said, "it's been a cup of
coffee or a casual drink and there's not a hint of a spark of
chemistry."

Be as forthcoming in your profile as you can. That way,
when you meet, you've done all you can to let this person know
about you. The chemistry is out of your control.

You've gathered some ideas about what is appealing
and what isn't. Still, you don't want your write-up to be like

anybody else's, so I'm going to give you some specific guidelines.

Take Plenty of Time

Take several hours or a whole day to do this. The reason you need to set aside plenty of time is that you are thinking and writing about yourself, and that's more difficult for some people than it is for me. I think about myself about 95% of the time. I'm one of those, "Enough about me. What do you think about me?" types. You may be just the opposite, but you are going to have to get over that when you begin to toot your own horn over the Internet.

Do not start this process when you're in a hurry or desperate for a date. Don't go on the Internet because it's Valentine's Day, and you won't, as usual, be receiving any candy or flowers. You just know you can score a valentine really quickly online. Not likely. Instead of panicking when you don't have a date for New Year's Eve, take New Year's Day to work out your profile.

Don't Tell Everything

You may have a compulsion to "tell it like it is" and not be concerned if you alienate your audience. If they can't handle the truth, that's their problem, right? Although I'm not suggesting you lie, it's a good idea to put your best foot forward, so to speak. We all want to make a good first impression, and that's the whole idea behind your profile. Your dates can discover the warts later. They have no place in your profile.

One headline stated, "Underachieving moody introvert seeking overachieving lady to balance her life." I thought this was very funny, but I'm not sure he meant it to be funny. He probably thought he was just being honest. He went on to say that he was a "bit of a loner" and could "get into a moody funk from time to time." Those qualities might apply to any one of us on occasion, but it's not really a good idea to share them with the world. Better to let the person you're dating find out for themselves.

Catherine, a feminine lady with a butch haircut, is allowing her extremely short hair to grow long because every, and I mean EVERY guy on the planet likes long hair. Does that sound too accommodating? I don't think so. She can get it cut as soon as she snags the guy. Seriously, your hair doesn't have to be down to your butt, just soft and touchable.

Ask a Friend for Help

Ask your best friend or ex-boyfriend (assuming you parted on friendly terms) what they like best about you. Ask yourself what you like best about you. Chances are, your potential date will like the same qualities. What accomplishments are you the proudest of? What obstacles have you overcome to become the person you are now? What are you good at—playing the piano, running a marathon, baking chocolate pies, making love?

Don't say you are "just an average Joe," or you are "no better nor worse than the next person." We all want someone special, and there's something special about all of us. It's your job to find those exceptional qualities in yourself, as hard as you may think it is. Use positive terms and phrases, like, "I'm kind, warmhearted and not afraid of public speaking," or "I like to cuddle in front of the fireplace, preferably with someone other than my Bichon Frise."

Be Specific

Another important rule: be specific. How many times has your English 101 teacher said that? You forget? Plenty, that's how many. Do not say you like to dine out, read and go to the movies. Be specific! "I love spicy Indian food, and my favorite restaurant is Kalachandji's. I read mysteries, but don't think Michael Connelly's *Bloodwork* made a very good movie. On the other hand, the movie, *Cold Mountain*, was much better than the book." Be specific!

The Sense of Humor Myth

What do you think is the most often requested quality? What quality does 99.99% of the population believe they have? *A good sense of humor.* For some reason, everyone thinks they have this quality, and I'm pretty sure, based on my past experiences, that they don't. There's really a goodly number of people in the United States of America who do not have, nor have they ever had, a good sense of humor. Many have no humor at all, and wouldn't recognize humor if it laid an egg on their head. If you don't have a sense of humor, don't say you do. On the other hand, don't say you don't either, because everyone is looking for that trait. And since everyone on the Internet says they have one, don't necessarily believe it. *Make them prove it!* If it's not evident in their profile, then they probably don't have one! You'll have to be amusing for both of you. And telling stupid jokes does not classify as a sense of humor. Humor is only funny if it is original.

I corresponded with a man who had participated and won numerous marathons, triathalons and I-don't-know-what-athons. Joseph never smiled in any of his pictures, but I suppose one doesn't feel much like smiling after running a marathon. After his second e-mail, I wrote him the following one:

> *You're such an accomplished man, I feel a little intimated. I have a friend who was a long distance runner in college, and he said the majority of it was mental. Some people have called me "mental," so you'd think I'd be able to run long distances, wouldn't you?*

I thought it was funny, but he never said a thing about it. Maybe it wasn't funny. Or perhaps I'm one of those people who think they have a sense of humor, but doesn't.

To Lie or Not to Lie

We've come to one of the unresolved conflicts in Internet dating, and it's also one of those things I've read that doesn't necessarily ring true. Everything I read states unequivocally that you should not lie about anything in your profile or in your later e-mails. But my contention is that if you don't fudge a little on your age (depending on how old you are), you may be cheating yourself out of some potential dates.

Here's why: I could pass for being ten years younger than my actual age. Few men under the age of sixty would even look at my ad because many of them are looking for younger women. Consequently, even though I would like to date a 40 to 45-year-old man, and wouldn't look ridiculous with one, if I didn't lie about my age, no 40 to 45-year-old would give me a second glance. When he's doing his search, he's going to be looking for women younger than him or not much older. There are exceptions to this. I received an e-mail from Kyle, a 25-year-old. I figured he must have been injured in the Iraqi War and thought a post-menopausal woman wouldn't mind as much.

So, should I or shouldn't I lie?

You might respond by saying that even though younger men might not find me, I would be able to perform a search and find them. I could take the initiative and write to them. Well, maybe, but I decided to lie. I avoided the men whose profiles specifically stated that honesty was the most important quality they were seeking in a woman.

Will my lies catch up with me? If so, what will be the consequences? Stay tuned for the next exciting episode of *Baby Boomer Bachelorette.*

There are a few things you should not lie about. If you're seventy-five and you look it, don't say you're fifty-five. If you never darken the door of the gym, and your middle shakes like a bowl full of Jell-O, don't say you're fit and toned. If you're fifty-five, don't say you'll only date women who are twenty-five.

On the Showtime series "Family Business," "Seymour Butts" is trying to Internet date. He becomes increasingly discouraged because every time he tells his dates what he does for a living, they lose interest. What is his business? He produces, directs, and sometimes stars in pornographic movies. Should he lie? Probably not. This is one of those situations where he should be honest even if it hurts.

Mary Anne, an attractive forty-nine year old, was meeting a forty-eight year old man for the first time. Over the phone he had told her things about himself, like he had a prominent family, but her search company could not confirm this. When she met him, she knew he'd either had a very hard life, or he'd lied about being forty-eight. He confessed that he was really fifty-three.

"And he looked fifty-three," Mary Anne said. Although she felt uncomfortable with his big stories, most of which she suspected weren't true, she did get curious when she didn't hear from him for a while. When she was finally able to reach him by telephone, he apologized for not getting in touch with her.

"He told me he had a mini-stroke," Mary Anne said, "but the only thing it had affected was his eye." I had this image of a fifty-three-year-old man with his bad eye hanging limp from disuse. I couldn't help but laugh. Who knew if he was telling the truth or not? If he wasn't, it certainly was an elaborate excuse for not calling.

If you have a good reason for lying, keep it simple.

Qualities Men Look for in Women

Research reveals the qualities men look for in women. The list reads like a *Who's Who of Women of Perfection*: the woman must be active, social, warmhearted, touchy-feely, even tempered, down-to-earth, doesn't nag or complain, and is a fun-lover . . . and, oh yeah, has a good sense of humor. That one certainly came as no surprise. I'd be willing to bet we all think we have the above characteristics, just like we think we have a good sense of humor. I'm sure I have all those traits, and now I'm going to make sure the gents online know it too.

I think they forgot to mention long, blonde hair, shapely legs that go all the way to her waist, perfect skin, sexually acrobatic, loves watching sports on TV, and the clincher—looks great without makeup. I'm a writer, and every male writer in my critique group describes their sexy heroines as looking great without makeup. No such thing in the real world. That's why they call it *fiction*.

Any of us would take that if we could get it. But we're trying to deal with reality here, and while it's not the movies, it's not all bad news either. The people looking for love on the Internet are basically like us. And we're lovable and desirable, aren't we?

As women grow older, we force ourselves to give up our girlish traits. Men seem to cherish and cling to theirs. They are always ready to play and have fun. Women need to hold onto those traits themselves. Men love a woman who is light-hearted, willing to abandon her dignity, and allow the child in her to come out.

I really liked Lincoln's profile, except that he wrote out that long laundry list I discussed before. It wasn't about his own qualities, however, but about what he wanted in a woman. I couldn't resist being a smart ass. I copied the list verbatim, and sent him this e-mail:

> *So you're 'looking for someone who is funny, intelligent, good looking, sexy, romantic, in good shape. Who is young hearted, good hearted and just fun to be with.' Does it have to be the same woman?*

I said I was kidding at the end of the e-mail, but I guess he didn't think it was too funny. I never heard from Lincoln again. Never receiving a reply from men happened to me often, and it probably will to you too. Don't become discouraged. Keep on sending those e-mails, and you'll soon be rewarded.

Qualities Women Look for in Men

What are over-fifty women looking for in men? Someone who can get an erection without taking Viagra? Not really. Women are looking for the same things as men. They just couch it in more esoteric terms, like, "a man who will honor me as I honor him," "someone who respects me for who I am," "a romantic guy who will do spur of the moment things to prove that he loves me"—that kind of stuff. It's all pretty generic. Any of it could apply to any of us at any given moment.

It's up to you to zero in on your best assets, and *please* find a way to tell our future hero about it in at least a somewhat original way.

Now you've isolated your best traits and found a tantalizing way to convey them on your profile. Consider what you are looking for in a man. Do you just want to have a few dates to the movies, or a long-term companion to keep you warm on cold nights? Do you want everlasting love, marriage, children? Don't laugh. Some of us aren't too old to bear children. As of this year (2004), the youngest Baby Boomers turned forty. Lots of women have babies in their forties. Or were you merely looking for a sex slave?

You can't get everything you want, but finding someone with many of your top-requested qualities is possible with some patience and persistence and a setting aside of ego. One caution: don't sound needy. There's no bigger turnoff than someone who is desperate (even if you are).

Do you have a big family, but aren't particularly interested in someone else's? Is your family small, like mine, and you'd love to be involved with a man who has a large family? Do you have children at home? You need to find someone who is willing to accept that situation.

Do not look for someone to support you, whether you are a man or a woman. If you're not financially solvent, it's best to get that way on your own. I often hear the trite suggestion that I find a man with money, and marry him so I would be set for life. That is a very strange suggestion given the fact that men with real money usually end up with supermodels. Why would someone with money want to marry me? Of course, I'm adventurous, caring, warmhearted, loving, excited about life . . . oops, I'm listing those traits the way I told you not to. The point is, I'm financially solvent, so I don't need someone to take care of me. But I would like someone who makes close to as much money as I do, and ideally, more. If that's what I want, that's what I should ask for.

Do you want a dreamer or someone with his feet firmly planted on earth? How about quiet and introspective or outgoing and gregarious? Someone passionate or compassionate? Many of the qualities you value and are looking for in other people are ones you possess yourself.

What about sex? Are you the "I prefer to cuddle" type (a type I've never been able to understand) or are you looking for the Big O every time, all the time (yeah!)? Make sure you let that be known, although not necessarily in those crass terms.

Are you a compromiser or a fighter? A planner or spontaneous? How important are any or all of these things to you? There's a lot of soul-searching involved in this and will give you a great opportunity to get to know yourself better. You will be able to narrow down and define who you are and what you want.

What about the biggie? Religion. Do you make it to church on holidays, or do you go every time the doors open?

Are you spiritual, but not religious? Are you an atheist? All important questions. Money is the thing that people most often argue about, but religion can either bring two people together or drive a huge wedge between them.

Profile Critique

Once you've written your ad, be sure to show it to a friend who can assess it for you, preferably a male friend if you're female, or a female friend if you're male. Even better, show it to someone who has experience in online dating, and ask them what they think.

Collette found a live-in boyfriend on-line. I asked Sam what drew him to her profile. He said her pictures were very pretty. (I took them, so I considered that a compliment.) He said she sounded like she'd be a lot of fun. He wasn't looking for marriage, and some of the ads sounded like the women were too serious.

Lessons from the Past

Being women who have lived a large part of our lives, we know more about ourselves and what we want from a relationship. Most of us have learned lessons from the past, and may be seeking something different from what we had then. I know I am.

I like to compare this to the time I was looking for property to buy, the aforementioned piece of green. Patches of green are quickly disappearing in the Dallas-Fort Worth area, as I'm sure it is everywhere in the United States. I found a piece of property in Midlothian (Texas) surrounded by farmland, with beautiful green trees, a small stream, and a tiny lake all its own, plus rolling hills—a scarcity in North Texas. I was on the verge of buying this thirty-eight acres, when I discovered that the cement plant (for which Midlothian is famous) owned all the land on three sides of my property. Within the next five to ten years, they were going to turn the land into rock quarries. Yikes! My beloved property was going to be surrounded by dynamite blasting, heavy truck traffic, and a barren, treeless pit.

Oh, how I wanted to cling to it, to remain faithful to it, to not let it go even though I knew it was flawed. I wanted to keep it so badly, I even thought I might be able to live with the noise, dust and chaos of a rock quarry.

Unlike my love life, common sense prevailed, and I found another piece of property with all the qualities I was looking for, which I bought because I used my head as well as my heart. There's a lesson in there somewhere, if you can decipher the analogy. You can find a man with all the qualities you're looking for without him being so flawed as to negate the possibilities of a long-term, intimate relationship. The lesson: You cannot live surrounded by a rock quarry and be happy.

Sample Profile

Below is my first profile. I'm giving it here to help you jump-start writing your own. Don't steal my profile verbatim, because it won't suit you. It's rather long and could be shortened some, but I'm in love with my own words, and hate cutting them.

I have an awarding-winning sense of humor. Really. My short story, "First Impressions," won the Katherine Anne Porter Humor Award. It was about over-forty dating and was based on a true experience. I've also written two novels and numerous other short stories, and keep my day job to support my writing habit. Contrary to the stereotypical writer-as-introspective-loner, I am quite the opposite. I'm extroverted and enjoy being around people. Be careful, though. You might end up in one of my novels!

I'm warmhearted, love animals of all kinds, and have a dog and a cat, both rescued from the streets.

I'm a movie nut, go at least once a week, and believe 'The Deer Hunter' is the greatest movie ever made. I catch every 'Trading Spaces' episode, and my beautiful home reflects my love of do-it-yourself home improvement.

My favorite sport is 4-wheel driving over mountain passes. Although I have an innate fear of heights, I adore mountains, and want to be above tree line whenever possible.

I embrace change in my life, and am looking for someone who's as adventurous and fun-loving as I am; a personable nonsmoker who cares about his health; an affectionate, financially stable guy who can hold his own in diverse company. My family is small, so your children and grandchildren would be welcome.

This profile emphasizes my strong points in an original way. I can prove I'm funny because I won a humor award. I'm an individual—not a stereotypical writer. I'm loving and kind because I rescue animals. It encompasses many of the traits people are looking for in their mates, i.e., active, adventurous, caring, compassionate, dynamic, fit, fun-loving, funny, healthy, kind, loving, smart, creative, warmhearted, etc. I merely *showed* how I was all those things rather than writing out a laundry list.

This profile has received many positive responses. Here are a few of them:

"If someone can't have a great time with you, then there's just lots wrong with them." "I couldn't help noticing your personal information. You are a very quality person." "I enjoyed your profile. You seem to be a wonderful woman."

It would not be fair to mention the above if I didn't tell you about the very first response I received: "Are you as horny as I am?" Since I didn't know who sent this, and therefore was not privy to how horny he was, I was unable to respond to his question. I chalked this one up as obscene and reported it to the website.

Not every website asks for the information in this form, and most of them want you to fill out a questionnaire. I would highly recommend doing that, as it leads to even more responses. Sometimes they're so long and involved, they get tedious, so be sure to set aside plenty of time to fill in the information.

Profile Revisions

The first version of our "script" will be followed by numerous revisions. I recommend that you update and revise your profile regularly, every week or two, if possible. That will keep it fresh and keep you higher up on the selections. After a few first responses, I found it necessary to add the phrasing, "I don't relate well to cowboy types and am not interested in hunters." For some reason, cowboys really like me.

I received an e-mail from Bobby, who wore his Stetson in every photograph. He was from Lamesa, which is in West Texas, so maybe he didn't know any better. I responded by telling him that I was sure he was a quality person, but I just couldn't get past the "cowboy thing." He wrote me back, saying,

> *What? You live in Texas and you can't get past the cowboy thing? But you know, I was gettin' tired of going to the family reunion to look for a girlfriend so I decided to try this here Internet thing and started winkin' at all them purdy girls. Well, 'Hee Haw' is about to come on so I better end this here letter to youse.*

I had to admire his sense of humor, and he certainly proved he had one, but not everybody in Texas is a cowboy, and certainly not in the D/FW area.

I made other adjustments as time passed, one of them being that I was looking for a partner who wanted a "fiery sensual relationship." I thought my too-literary, high-blown profile needed a dash of sex, just like any good novel.

If all this photograph and profile business is too much for you to handle, and you have some extra cash around the house, there are people out there who are willing to help you or completely do it for you for the right price. I've listed a few of their websites in the *Resources* section at the end of this book.

Now we have our script, and it's time to move on to the next step in our preproduction stage of development.

15. The Production Schedule

It's time to draw up a tentative schedule for the production, that is, deciding how much time we're going to devote to finding a date. By now you should know exactly what you're looking for, whether it's just a date or someone to travel with, a long-term relationship or marriage. Defining your goals was addressed earlier, but it should not be skipped over lightly. It will directly affect how much time you're going to spend on this project.

If you're strictly looking for marriage, then you might want to screen your potential dates more thoroughly than you would if you are merely looking for a play-buddy to go to the movies with once a week. Statistics show that Baby Boomers are wary of marriage because about 15.4% of all Americans in their fifties are divorced. Also, second marriages tend to end quickly. Consider shacking-up before you take the matrimonial plunge.

If all you want is a really good-looking guy to show off to your girlfriends or your ex-husband, then you don't need to know much more than that they look good in their photograph (which can be deceiving, as we learned earlier).

Like any other important goal in life, this will require a lot of work and time on your part if it's going to be successful. We always make time for the things that are priorities in our lives. A few activities may have to be temporarily set aside in order to make our production successful. Nothing like sending the kids to your ex-husband's for six months, or putting your mother in a nursing home until you've landed the man of your dreams—nothing that drastic.

Making Sacrifices

You will have to make a few sacrifices. Like taking less time to watch reality shows on television, or stop going out for fattening dinners with people you don't even like, because you don't have anything else to do.

The first thing I did was set up a special e-mail box for the sole purpose of receiving e-mails from potential dates. It is totally separate from my other personal e-mail, which I use for friends and business. I also have an e-mail at work, which I never use for anything except company business. I would definitely not recommend getting your dating e-mails at work. They probably aren't being, but can be, read by administrative personnel. Don't let the boss catch you doing this, unless you want to lose your job in this troubled market.

I set aside some time right after I come home from work and exercise, just before dinner, to take care of my personal e-mails. Sometimes it takes fifteen minutes, sometimes two hours. Depends on the number and the necessity of a detailed response. You may receive more than I do if you're younger, prettier and thinner. You probably will, so you will need to devote more time to it. The longer your profile is on a certain dating site, the less responses you will receive. The holidays are the exception to this. No one wants to be alone on Christmas Day and everyone makes a fresh resolution on New Year's.

How thoroughly should you read and decipher the object of your affection's profiles? I'm sure profiles are important, and they will tell you much about the person (even ones that are sparse in the information department), but the truth is some people are just better at communicating through the written word than others. Some have dedicated more thought, time and energy to the composition of their profile, so you'll have to decide for yourself, based on the individual profile, how much weight to attach to it.

This is why I think it's important that your profile be as revealing as possible. It will help the other party decide quickly whether you are most likely compatible with them. On the other hand, one little thing in a profile can be off-putting, even if you've liked the person very much up to that point.

Being Too Specific

Being too specific can be as difficult as not being specific enough, although not as common. Tye sounded like someone I would be attracted to, until he said he wanted a woman whose legs went all the way to her waist. I don't know how many women would fit that description, but I'll bet not many. If that were true about a woman, I'd suggest that she describe herself that way, but a man should not be that demanding in his profile. Conversely, a woman shouldn't ask for a man with washboard abs either. How many hits do you think she would get? Even if the guy were sporting a six pack, would he want a woman who sounded so shallow?

Here's Janet's response to that ad: "I'd like a guy whose dick goes all the way to his knees, too, but that doesn't mean I'm going to find him." Perhaps I should put that in the "What I'm Looking For" portion of my profile.

Even if you are shallow, try not to sound as if you are in your profile.

How much time are you going to devote to e-mailing someone before you decide to meet them? There's no definitive answer to this. It will be determined by your personality type, and your common sense. A few e-mails would be sensible, if merely to find out if they are a nut case, and it probably won't take too many to find this out. Here's a sample of one of my nutcases. I don't really understand most of this e-mail, which explains why he's probably a nutcase:

> *I can talk about sex to my pets let alone some people who I don't respect as much as them. Sex is fun right? Are you as good at it as me? Don't we all want to be satisfied? All I know is I can satisfy women better than most women can satisfy me.* (So far he just sounds like a braggart, and the sex talk is inappropriate.) *What does that say about our deepest darkest desires? Especially down in Brokenheartsville. Here's to the girl who wrecked my world. I don't drive a coup de ville* (sic) *but I have a Chevy truck. I am shameless!*

Perhaps he was making obscure literary references or quoting song lyrics, but I didn't get them. He sounded like a kook to me, and I never e-mailed him again. Luckily, he wasn't an e-mail stalker type.

When do you agree to meet them for the first time? Once you begin dating, you will be going to different places and meeting strange people (perhaps I should have just said "strangers"). Getting to know someone takes time. If you are like me, your life is already pretty full, so something will have to give. In my case, it was reading and watching television, both things I love. While I didn't stop doing them entirely, I was forced to cut down on my habit.

It all depends on what your goals are. You are probably going to spend more time with a potential husband than you are a buddy who likes to take you dancing for the exercise.

If you've been diligent in your soul-searching and know what you want, you can eliminate in the first few rounds of e-mails the ones who are not right for you. Then comes the fun part—meeting them in person—but not yet!

16. Key Personnel and Key Locations

Who are you going to include on your team for support? This is an important question. I told you in the previous chapter that there were some activities we might have to give up in order to spend more time achieving our production goals—the successful presentation of *Baby Boomer Bachelorette* to a receptive audience.

Touchstone

Don't stop exercising, eating right, going to work or communing with close friends and family. They are the ones you are going to be relying on as your touchstones when you do actually begin dating. You will need someone who knows where you are going, with whom, and when to expect you home.

My sister is my touchstone. When I'm meeting a new man, I tell her exactly where I'm going when I meet him. I make sure she knows the address, and I always take my cellphone in case she wants to call me to check out how I'm doing, or I want to call her for an excuse to get away. I leave their full names and telephone numbers with her at all times. If your potential dates won't give you that information, do not meet them!

What about out-of-state dates? I avoid them like the plague. It would require too much time, effort and money to initiate and maintain a long-distance relationship. I don't mind running all over the D/FW Metroplex, but I draw the line at another state. For some reason, men in Oklahoma just love me. Aren't there any female Baby Boomers in OK?

Daniel told me he had dated a woman from Tulsa. He said she came down to Texas every other weekend, but he never made it to Tulsa. He discovered she had no intention of ever moving to Texas, and he had no intention of moving to Tulsa, so he ended the inconvenient relationship. What would be the point? People need to spend time together in order to further their relationship. Being together is necessary to create a history. Sharing experiences is what cements a relationship.

An exception to the long-distance rule would be if you travel often or plan to move to another city anyway. You could use that as an opportunity to broaden your search area.

I like to meet guys at the Barnes & Noble so we can have coffee and look at books. It helps me find out a few things about the person. Unfortunately, the lighting in the Barnes & Noble store isn't very flattering. I'm looking for a candle-lit venue with something to do other than eat. If the guy wants to go somewhere different, I make sure my touchstone is informed of that fact.

Be Safe and Careful

ALWAYS meet a new man in a public place. NEVER be without your own transportation. KEEP your cellphone charged at all times. CONTINUE this practice for several meetings until your common sense (and possibly an Internet search on the person) tells you he is okay. Actually, some of our common sense is swept aside when the love chemical hits our systems, so an Internet search would probably be better if you think you might be serious about this person.

Yes, there are lots of nut cases in the world, but if that type is attracted to you or you're attracted to them, you're just as likely to meet them in the real world as in cyberspace.

Be aware of the married-and-cheating types. If you want to pursue the relationship, and he is never willing to show you his place, he's probably married. Run the other way as quickly as possible.

Test Drive Your Profile

Now is the time to decide on which matchmaking websites you are going to post the incredibly original profile you've created.

No one is paying me to tout their website, like Yahoo Personals paid Bob Guiney of "The Bachelor," so I have no intention of telling you any one is better than the other. The ones that work best for you are found through experimentation and diversity. They can be accessed based on location, age or religion (I know there's a Jewish one), or body type (tall, large size, etc.), sexual preferences, lifestyle (there's actually one for recovering addicts and alcoholics). Almost all of them will give you a free test drive, and I think that's just great.

I took advantage of that opportunity, and test drove my ad on a site that allowed me to put myself into the "silver" category. I cannot over-emphasize this: DO NOT PUT YOURSELF INTO THAT CATEGORY IF YOU'RE A BABY BOOMER. We are not seniors now, and I'm beginning to doubt if we ever will admit that we're old. I don't intend to admit to being old until I'm at least a hundred.

Apparently, not very many people wanted to admit to being "Silver." I counted maybe ten women in my age group who allowed themselves to be put into that category, and even fewer men. The pickings were sparse. Very few men are going to be looking at your profile if you place yourself in the wrong category. You're a Baby Boomer. You are not old!

Only use websites that have photographs. You must know what the person looks like. Perhaps, since I'm a highly visual person, that means more to me than it does to you, but it is quite tedious to read hundreds of personal ads without photographs, and try to decipher what the person is all about. A photograph could keep you from wasting a lot of time. I'm not talking about just trying to find someone good looking, but maybe you have an aversion to bald guys, or maybe your boss has a little nose, and you therefore prefer men with big noses. There's nothing wrong with that.

If he says he's a cuddly bear type, count on it, he's overweight. I personally would prefer that a guy have some excess weight in his gut rather than be short and skinny, so that would be okay with me, but some women prefer skinny men.

One service gives you a test to discover what physical type you prefer. Of course, I preferred a "very handsome man" with a chiseled jaw who was younger than forty-five. Most men, I'm sure, picked the "long blond hair" type with a heart-shaped or oval face and younger than thirty-five. Who wouldn't? I didn't think much of this test, because it didn't really say who we wanted to date, unless it was a fashion model or movie star. Leave those physical types for your sexual fantasies. Unless you're rich or famous, be more realistic.

Which Services to Sign Up With

The websites charge monthly rates to respond to ads. The fees vary, but will most likely be around $25 per month. I don't think that's too much. The problem may occur when you can't decide which one to utilize. Give all the major ones a try, and then make your decision. It's possible to be on more than one, and if you have the time and the money, that would be great. I found, especially at first, that I had enough responses just being on one to last me for a long time. Once the initial responses began to grow smaller, as they will after you've been on for a few months, I included another website.

As we've discussed, don't sign up with anything that makes you a "silver" or a "senior." "Baby Boomer" is okay, because that's what you are. You're most likely proud of it and looking for another Baby Boomer. There are some exclusively for over-forty and Baby Boomers, and it's okay to make use of these although they do frequently use the dreaded term "senior." I've listed a few of them in the Resources section at the end of the book.

Speed Dating

Speed dating is featured on some websites for meeting singles. My first speed dating experience was with Cassie, a friend. We went to a local restaurant, were given numbers and a tabulation sheet. We were both at the same table, but with different numbers. About twenty other women were at the event. The men were given numbers also, and they made the rounds of the tables, having about four minutes to speak with each woman. At the end of the meet, we circled "yes," "no," or "maybe" by the man's number to indicate if we were interested in him or not. The scores were tabulated, and we were notified by e-mail if we made a mutual match (both of you circled "yes" or "maybe"). They also let you know if someone was interested in you (he circled "yes" or "maybe" but you didn't).

The whole thing was so screwed up that I got a mutual match from two guys who I had not only circled "no" to, but had written "yuk!" by their names. The same thing happened to Cassie. So, if you attend one of these events, be sure it's run properly.

Just a warning: the women exceeded the men by at least a third, although I'm told the organizers attempt to equalize it. If you don't like a lot of competition, this wouldn't be the proper event for you to attend. Of course, Cassie and I both thought we were by far the best looking women in the place. The men didn't seem to agree, even when I told them so. Next time, we're getting the event organizers to separate us, like you would two unruly kids. Cassie claimed that the two of us together might be too overwhelming for these guys.

Try the most popular dating sites first. There's probably a reason why they're the most popular. Take as many as you want for a test drive, and see if their format fits your personality.

17. Dress Rehearsals

We've made ourselves into the best we can be at the moment, delved into our souls and put our deepest thoughts into words, broadcasted on the greatest "network" (website) we can find, and put on our best face in terrific photographs for our potential dates to view. We are physically and emotionally ready to put our egos on the line. Most of the prep work is done, and there are only a few more steps to take. We're sitting on our laurels and waiting for the hundreds of responses that are bound to come our way. We have entered the world of cyber-dating and can't wait for our lives to change. They will change, won't they?

Well . . . that depends . . . on a lot of things. It depends mostly on how much time, thought and talent you've put into your profile and photograph, and it depends on how much time you're willing to invest in the process of Internet dating. It probably won't be enough just to post your photo and profile and wait. You may have to go looking for yourself. Use the site's search feature to find men who might not have noticed you, but with whom you feel you would be compatible.

Take Advantage of Opportunities

Most of the better websites have lots of different ways of introducing potential mates to each other, and I would suggest taking advantage of them. This will once again require more time, but what price is a compatible companion worth? Isn't it just as important as buying a new car or deciding whether to subscribe to cable or satellite? You should at least invest as much time looking for, analyzing and communicating with your potential dates as you do investigating new cars.

Lower Expectations

If you're not getting the kind of responses you expected, welcome to the real world. Expectations are usually much higher than they should be because we think cyberspace is magic, and we'll be receiving millions of offers from the most fabulous of men. Was that happening to you *before* you went online?

In my twenties, I worked as a court clerk for Dallas County. I met hundreds of men under the age of forty (attorneys, of course). I was young, attractive and available, and had discovered a dating smorgasbord. My early thirties were spent in the swinging singles bars of Dallas, and I wasn't exactly dateless then either.

Then I hit forty, divorced and once again single, and what do you think happened then? Well, I really don't want to talk about it. Oh, okay, I will for you.

I've already said I was dumped by my boyfriend Jake. I had also quit smoking, which caused me to eat constantly, and I was getting fat. For the next ten years, I was more or less in a trance. I was nearly fifty before I started getting myself back together again. It was a slow process. I'm not a fast learner like you probably are.

Therefore, I can't really tell you what it would be like to be a normal forty-to-fifty-year-old looking for dates, although I'm sure it's more difficult than it was during the twenties and thirties. Not nearly as difficult, though, as not trying at all.

Don't expect the world, and you won't be disappointed. As with all goals that are worth attaining, be persistent. Every failure means you're one step closer to success. That's something every self-help guru in the world will tell you, and they'll tell you that because it's true.

Persistence

My sister has a dog named Sweet Face. She is my role model when it comes to persistence. Sweet Face wants to be inside the house, even when my sister is not there. She has a nice, air conditioned garage to go into and almost an acre for a back yard. But that's not good enough. She'd rather be lying up on my sister's comfortable sofa rather than outside with the other dogs. So she persistently bites through chainlink fence until she has a hole big enough to crawl through. When that's done, she has to squeeze her large-size body through a medium-sized doggie door. No matter how many times the fence is repaired, no matter how many teeth she loses, no matter what barriers are placed in her path, including an electrified wire, Sweet Face eventually ends up back inside the house.

Like Sweet Face, we are most likely going to have to work for what we want. It may be a long, arduous process, and quite often discouraging. Most dogs or people would have quit long before my sister's dog did, long before they were even inside the fence, much less before attempting to squeeze through the too-small doggie door.

Did I say *persistence*. Let me repeat—persistence. If you already have this virtue, nurture it and keep it safe. If you don't have it, acquire it. It's the one thing that will keep you going when things seem hopeless.

Rejection

Can you handle rejection? That's what Amanda wanted to know when I interviewed her about Internet personals. I get rejected every day of my life when I receive rejection letters from agents saying they aren't interested in my novel.

But that's not the same thing, Amanda told me. When they're rejecting your novel, it's not personal. When a date is rejecting you, it is. It feels personal, I said. Regardless, you are going to get rejected, and it's going to hurt, and you're going to have to get past it, and do it all over again. Sorry, that's just the way it is.

On the other hand, you're going to have lots of fun, meet new and interesting people, do things you've never done before (not necessarily kinky sex, unless that is the kind of website you belong to), and be uplifted with personal fulfillment and admiration from someone you care about. That sounds worth the sacrifice, doesn't it?

We've taken the production out for a test drive, a dress rehearsal. We've taken advantage of the trial offers from various online dating services and picked the one or two or three on which we are going to permanently place our profile—or until we find our significant other, whichever comes first.

It is time to put this production on the air, see if all our hard work has paid off, and find out what the results will be.

PRODUCTION
♀

18. First Date

Before you have your first date, you're going to be communicating with numerous potential dates, assuming you don't find one your first time out. The names and information can get confusing, and, if you're like me, your memory isn't reliable enough to retain it all.

Getting Organized

You might need a filing system to keep all these men straight. I'm a legal secretary, so I like to make file folders. I made up one for the men I rejected and one for the ones with whom I intended to continue corresponding. I printed out their e-mails and placed them in the appropriate folder. If I was having phone contact with them, I put their phone numbers on the printouts with their pictures, and put them in my purse. That way, when my cellphone rang, I would know which one of them was calling.

You can divide the responses up in a more complicated system if you prefer, or even rate them, if you want, but my system was less work. You might want to make a folder of the ones you actually had a date with, which would separate them from the other positive responses that ultimately went nowhere. I have quite a few of those. Or you might want to acquire an accordion folder with each section divided as a letter of the alphabet and file them alphabetically. Use whichever system works best for you. My problem with the accordion folder is that they aren't divided into rejections and acceptances.

Once you have established a short e-mail correspondence with someone you like, proceed to telephone communication. Do not spend the rest of your life e-mailing. If you communicate well on the telephone, then make a quick-meet date. Do not continue to have long telephone conversations. You're looking for a companion, not a girlfriend.

Harvey, with whom I spoke on the phone, possibly did not understand my sense of humor. I told him I had a close relationship with my sister, and if a man wanted to marry me, he'd probably have to marry my sister, too. Here's what he wrote to me:

I enjoyed our talk on Sunday. I went back and reviewed your profile. You are attractive in an unusual kind of way.

What does "attractive in an unusual kind of way" mean?

But I wondered where you have time for anyone. Your work/car pooling seems to negate any weekday visits. Your Sundays—at least mornings seem to be locked up with friends. And you seem to have planned the rest of your life to include living with your sister at Lake Waxahachie.

Here is my response:

I was just engaging in all those activities to fill up my empty life until I met a man, but I'm perfectly willing to give them all up now that I've met you!

Of course, I told Harvey I was kidding, but perhaps he did not get my sense of humor. I assured him I always had time in my life for someone special. It seemed to have appeased him. Oh, and here's how he explained the crack about my "unusual attractiveness."

Yes, I do think that you are attractive as I said. All American? Perhaps. An interesting mix of professional-looking, girl next door and mystery.

I can live with that.

Exercise Caution

A few words of caution before we proceed. There are a lot of weirdos and nuts out there, many of them more than willing to take advantage of the Internet. You must exercise care, caution and good sense when dealing with strangers. And, even though they may seem familiar, and we think we've gotten to know them, everyone we meet on the matchmaking websites are strangers. You need to treat them as if they were strangers.

Take things very, very slowly. It's hard to believe someone with whom you have a tremendous amount of chemistry is actually a shyster and a con. That's why I recommend you introduce a friend or relation into the situation as soon as possible. Someone who's a good bullshit detector would be the best person to employ as your troubleshooter and objective observer—your touchstone.

We feel chemistry because of a drug our bodies produce, which accounts for the romantic feeling and the fact that we are totally unobjective. No one on drugs is a reliable source for anything, and you should consider yourself under the influence. If you have doubts, ask a research company to investigate the person you've singled out (or has singled out you). The company is not affected by your oxytocin level. However, this may not be enough. Sometimes it takes a stalker awhile to reach full bloom. You may have caught them merely in the budding stage.

This is why you need the objective third person, someone who has a vested interest in your well-being. I'm not trying to scare you. You could attract a freakazoid anywhere, but just be careful. Don't give out your address or telephone number online. Don't respond to any e-mail that makes you feel uncomfortable in any way, and report obscene e-mails to your Internet provider. If you have a cellphone, use that number for prospective dates. They can't find out where you are through your cellphone.

Reduce your expectations. If you've decided you'll settle for no one but Pierce Brosnan, you're going to be disappointed. Even if you have no movie star in mind, but a rigid set of qualities and standards the poor guy must live up to, you're going to be disappointed. Brenda refused to date anyone who wasn't an "earth" astrological sign. If you adhere to this standard, you're going to be disappointed. Cast a wide net, and you will be rewarded with lots of nibbles. Then you can start narrowing down your selections.

Don't come off as too desperate. If you cling to someone who is inappropriate, will you be any better off than if you were alone? Being alone with yourself—someone you at least like (we hope)—is much better than having to constantly squelch your needs and desires just to have a warm body next to you. You could hire an escort if that's all you wanted.

Believe in yourself. You are at a point in your life where you know more than you've ever known. You're happier, smarter, more accepting of yourself and others, more willing to experiment sexually, and probably more fun because you've learned not to take life too seriously. Have confidence. You're the best you've ever been.

One website I signed up with allowed the other person to send you a "Wink," which basically meant they were attracted to you but were too cowardly or didn't want to take the time to write you an e-mail. If you're not interested in the person winking at you, do not send them a polite e-mail indicating that. It may be the way your mother taught you to respond, but it instigates more e-mails with arguments as to why you should like them. To give a reason is to encourage argument.

Leonard sent me a wink, and when I went to his profile, it showed him holding up a fish he had just caught. Being an animal lover, I found this upsetting, so I wrote him back and told him I wouldn't be compatible with someone who fished. He countered with the fact that the fish was happily swimming downstream right after the picture was taken. Personally, I don't care. I still wasn't interested. I discovered not replying at all is the best course of action if you don't want to spend the rest of your life e-mailing people you have no intention of meeting.

However, this is a point of disagreement amongst others. Several men have protested when women do not give them a polite refusal. Personally, I think the fact that I did not respond is a polite refusal. And it saved us both a lot of time and energy. I have received e-mails several times from the same person to whom I have not responded, but I think they're just not getting the broad hint. I'll leave this up to your discretion, but I think you'll find that most will argue with you if you tell them you're not interested. Unless I just attract the argumentative type.

Now you are ready to meet someone for the first time. You have answered their e-mail, you both like each other's photographs and profiles, and you've determined a public place in which you both can conveniently meet. Most importantly, you've let your touchstone know exactly who you're meeting, where you're meeting him, what time, and when to expect you home. Hopefully, there will be a follow-up phone call to tell your support person that you arrived home safely.

Hit-and-Runs

This is the big event. You haven't had a date in ten years. What do you wear, how do you act, what do you do? Robin De Luca, author of *The Cyber-Dating Guru's Guide to Online-Dating*, referred to these first meetings as "drive-bys," and suggested you give each one of them no more than twenty minutes. It's not a date. It's merely a quick meeting to see if you want to carry it to the next level.

I describe them as "hit-and-runs." It could get messy. I'm usually all apprehensive and doubtful. I'm too fat, I think, my neck looks like an iguana's, my stomach looks like I swallowed a soccer ball—all looks issues which shows how shallow I am.

There is, however, another underlying issue. I'm uncomfortable because I'm disturbing the status quo. I'm forcing myself out of my comfort zone. It's too much trouble, I'm telling myself, and I wish I could just call the whole thing off. I want to go back to being the way I was. I needed to drop ten more pounds before I did this.

At this point, I remind myself that I was ten pounds thinner when I met the writer in California, and didn't feel any more confident than I do now. The problem is fear of change. Change is always uncomfortable at first.

Another reason I call it a hit-and-run, is by the time I'm through with the guy, he doesn't know what hit him. If I'm hitting him with the questions I've listed below, you can bet he's thinking he's been involved in a train wreck. I usually wait to ask him the big ones until the second or third date.

What to wear to the hit-and-run is obvious, or it would seem so to me. Didn't your mother always tell you to wear clean underwear in case you were in a car wreck? Wear something that is flattering and appropriate for the place you are meeting your new friend. I always stick to classic fashions, but you may have a different personal style than me.

Is "Be Yourself" Good Advice?

How do you act? I'm always hesitant to say "be yourself." I've never considered that very good advice. Who else could you be anyway? Even if you're trying to be somebody else, you're still yourself imitating somebody else. What if you're shy and retiring when you first meet someone, but come out of your shell after you get to know them? Getting to know the person you're meeting is the whole objective of this adventure. What if you're A.D.D. and talk constantly? You may have to force yourself to talk more or restrain yourself from talking too much.

Don't worry about asking too many personal questions. I have the type of personality that wants to know what makes another person tick—not just what he does for a living, where he goes on vacation, how many and how old are his kids, and does he have a dog or a cat. I like to ask the probing questions. People love to talk about themselves, and won't be offended regardless of what you ask them. If they don't want to answer, they won't. I've rarely asked a personal question that the other party wasn't eager to answer.

To make it easy for you, I've listed here a few artsy-fartsy questions you might want to ask your date, assuming you don't mind risking them thinking you're some kind of New Age nutcase. Uh, nothing against New Agers, just that most of us are on a slightly different plane than they. Don't monopolize the conversation, however, and give them a chance to ask you questions also.

Here goes:

1.   If you could relive one day in your life, which one would it be? Yes, this can include a past life when you were a Samurai warrior.

2.   Who was the greatest influence on your life and why? Please exclude comic book superheroes.

3.   Describe your relationship with your parents. Your children. Your companion animals.

4.   Do you love your job, or are you just biding time until you retire? What would you prefer to be doing to earn money?

5.   What do you like best about yourself?

6.   Do you believe in love at first sight, or do you believe love is something two people grow into?

I don't think anyone would be too insulted if you asked them the preceding questions, but on the other hand, they're rather generic and nonspecific.

When I went to the speed-dating soiree, the brochure suggested the following question: "If you could be an article of clothing, what would it be and why?" Did I feel stupid asking a man that question? Who? Me? The person who thought it up *should* have felt stupid. The guy who answered it *should* have felt stupid. His favorite article of clothing was a hula skirt, and he gave me a long and boring history of why the hula skirt meant so much to him.

Below is a list of questions I'd like to ask them. If you're a wimp, stick to the first set of questions. If you're daring and adventurous, see how these babies fly:

Questions to Ask Only if You Never Want to See Him Again

1.   Do you take Viagra?

I think that's a legitimate question, although some might be insulted to be asked. I don't really want a guy who has to rely on a drug to have an erection, although I understand that's pretty common after the age of fifty. If they had been eating their fruits and vegetables, they wouldn't be in this dilemma. To me, it's about the same thing as having to nurse some guy who hasn't taken care of himself. If you don't feel the same way, or you're squeamish, it's okay to avoid this question like a date with halitosis. Remember, these are my questions and concerns.

2.   Do you like animals? Do you think it's wimpy to have a cat?

Here's another one that some guys might be reluctant to answer. If they say they like animals, it would be a good idea to make sure they don't mean to eat or to have intercourse with.

The reason for the specific one about cats is that some men have taken it into their heads to dislike cats. Apparently, they think that's macho, just like their outdoor grilling. I put these two things on the same level, because outdoor grilling of animal products is the least macho thing a man can do, as discussed earlier. Liking cats can be quite macho, because a cat is an animal who is very discriminating in who they like, and if they like you, that means you must be pretty special.

Men, however, usually prefer dogs. I believe that's because dogs are more subservient and obsequious, and men want their companions to have these qualities. Watch out, ladies! They might expect that in their women, too.

That brings up another good question: "Do you like your women weak and dependent or strong and independent." That's a tricky one. They'll all say "strong and independent," because they think that's what you want to hear. But ask them about the cat versus dog situation, and you'll find out the real truth.

3.   Are you physically personable, or are you afraid if you touch me, I'll break?

If the man asks permission to touch or kiss you, run the other way immediately. Guys: no woman wants a man to ask permission to do something she's dying for him to do, so don't be a wuss and ask permission. You're an adult, not a little boy.

4.   Who do you fantasize about when you're masturbating?

Maybe not the best question to ask on the hit-and-run. Save it for a second or third date. By that time, I'm ready to find out everything about them sexually. Probably before that, but I try to restrain myself. If you want to get married, restrain yourself for at least a month. The longer you withhold sex, the more likely he is to end up marrying you. That's what the latest research tells us anyway.

This reminds me of something I put in my test profile on a website that had a long questionnaire they wanted you to fill out. One of their questions was: "What is 'SEXY'? What do you find 'SEXY' in a partner?" Here's the way I answered it (after I had also answered the question, "What's your favorite indoor activity," with "Sex"):

I find someone who is affectionate and personable to be sexy; someone who is exuberant about life; who is sexually assertive (doesn't ask permission to kiss me); someone

who can 'make-out' without it always leading to
sex, but who enjoys making love often.

This apparently caught more than one guy's eye, and the responses I got to it were basically the same: "I liked the part where you said that it was nice to make out without it always leading to sex. Many men just don't get that, do they? There's something to be said for what I think is the declining art of kissing and sensuality, don't you?" and "I love loving a woman who appreciates a caress, a touch, a tender kiss . . . . Don't get me wrong, I'm not afraid of passionate lovemaking. I'm willing to wait for that special moment."

On the surface, those responses sound nice, but they worried me. Why? It made me think that perhaps they were unable to have erections without long bouts of lovemaking, and that made me nervous. I'm not sure I'm capable of being patient with someone who's unable to perform. That seems mean, since the major fear men over forty have is their inability to perform. Women's major fear is being naked. You would rationalize that if they can forgive the way I look naked, then I should be able to forgive them for not being able to achieve erections every thirty seconds like a teenager. In theory, this is true. But my problem is that I think their lack of an erection is due to the fact that I'm naked.

5.   Should the toilet paper be hung with the end over or under?

There's a lot of controversy and debate regarding this subject, and it's just too controversial for me to take a position on in this book. Only you can decide for yourself. Give it a lot of thought and study before you make your decision. It also brings up the next question, which is very much a test of male sensitivity.

6. Do you know how disconcerting it is to wake up in the middle of the night and have both butt cheeks hit cold water because SOMEONE did not put the toilet seat down?

This is a "I can feel your pain" question that it is imperative a man answer in the affirmative, or you will be having compatibility issues for the rest of your lives.

7. Which of the following two things would you prefer to do on Saturday night: have sex with your girlfriend who's dressed up in a high school cheerleader uniform or watch soccer on a plasma TV?

This is a trick question, and if the man answers "I can do both at the same time," then you know he's a guy who is a diplomat and knows how to compromise and keep you happy.

8. When were you released from prison?

Another trick question. Note, we didn't say, "Have you ever been to prison?" which would immediately tip him off and give him an opportunity to lie. We merely, in a conversational tone, asked him for his release date.

9. Who is your best friend and why?

If he says "mother," I'd suggest asking for the check and leaving. If he says, "my dog, Biff," he's okay, except he probably talks baby talk to Biff. I don't have a problem with talking baby talk to your companion animals, because I do the same thing. However, this might strike some people as odd. They would perhaps believe that, since Biff is incapable of a verbal response, it would be a one-sided conversation. Ergo, the object of their affection is actually talking to himself. If he says his ex-wife is his best friend, ask for the check and leave. If he says, "John, whose life I saved when we served together in Vietnam," pay the check and suggest a motel room.

10.   If we make love, will you agree to use a condom?

Very important question. You'd be surprised how many men want to have sex without them. Grace, an urban woman living in a downtown loft, made a date with a raging cowboy type. The ones who wear the entire get-up—Stetson, cowboy-cut shirt, wide belt with rodeo belt buckle (and usually a belly hanging over it), boot-cut jeans, and shit-kickers (boots with pointy toes). All of which should have been a warning to her in the first place. He was already having trouble getting an erection, but finally accomplished the task. She requested he wear a condom before putting his waning penis inside her. He said he didn't want to because he didn't think he'd be able to maintain his erection.

Don't fall for that one, girls. Give it up for the time being, but do not have unprotected sex. Wait until you know more about the man, and until you both have had an HIV test. Hurrah for Grace! She refused to have intercourse with the cowboy, and made him compensate by giving her oral.

Maybe I was joking about the last ten questions, and maybe I wasn't. I would probably ask them of someone who appeared to have a similar sense of humor to mine. But if I'm out with someone who seems to take himself very seriously, I probably wouldn't. Unlikely I'd be out with someone who takes himself too seriously. You have to admit they'd really keep the conversation going . . . or bring it to a screeching halt.

These lists of questions would forever quell men's complaints that women are not forthright and direct enough about what they want and how they feel. Men apparently feel as if women are incapable of being honest and saying what's on their minds. It's the biggest complaint they have against us, and I think they're right. Don't give them subtle clues. How many men do you know who can pick up on them? Say what you're thinking and feeling outright. I doubt if you're going to put them off. And what if you did? Isn't it better to know that sooner than later?

Don't Waste Each Other's Time

Dating can be expensive, especially for Boomer men, many of whom still feel it's the man's job to pay the check. We can help out by cutting to the chase and asking the relevant questions, thereby sorting the keepers from the ones we throw back. Dating's also expensive on women. What about all those clothes and beauty care products? Consider sharing the expenses. Long gone are the days when men were supposed to pay for everything.

Let's don't waste each other's time. Men want someone who makes her man a priority in her life, and is a positive influence on his. Matthew said he wanted to be someone's hero, and I think a lot of men want that. I can remember what my ex-husband used to say. He thought I was too independent, and complained that I never let him do anything for me. At the time,

I didn't understand why that was a problem, but I do now. It makes them feel wanted and needed.

By the way, do not go into an extended monologue regaling your date with your numerous medical conditions. Major turn-off! And do not tell too much too soon. It's not necessary to make a complete confession about your checkered past the first few times you meet them. If it appears to be getting more serious, then would be the time to unburden your soul, but only on a need-to-know basis. You do not have to tell anyone everything unless it has a direct bearing on your relationship. Going into long stories about the hundreds of guys you've had kinky sex with will merely give your new love interest the wrong idea, even if you tell him it was the late sixties, early seventies, and you were under the influence of drugs.

Another word of caution. If a guy (or gal) is pushing you too far too fast, and you're feeling uncomfortable, back off. If they're not answering any of your questions, and won't be specific about their backgrounds, their jobs or where they live, back off. If they're too possessive, fly off the handle too quickly, or get too depressed too often and expect constant sympathy, back off.

E-mail your research company and have them checked out. Your personal safety is the most important thing, and fatal attractions aren't fun or interesting except in the movies.

Use your hit-and-runs for the purpose they are intended. When the thirty minutes to an hour is up, then you should leave. I'm not necessarily saying if you like the guy that you shouldn't prolong the date, but make it evident from the very beginning that it's going to only be for a short period of time. If you change your mind during the course of the date, you can still do that. If you continue the date longer than planned, do not forget to notify your touchstone. But if you want to make a quick exit, you've already laid the groundwork to be able to do that.

If everything works out the way we hope it will, then you and your new friend are ready to move to the next level.

When You Don't Click

What if it doesn't turn out the way you had hoped? You are going to have to write an e-mail telling the person you're not interested. That is, unless he freaks the minute he sees you, flees to the men's room, and never comes back out.

The following is a short, gentle e-mail I devised for the purpose of discontinuing the relationship:

> *It was nice to meet you and spend a little time talking to you. You are an attractive, charming man. Unfortunately, I did not feel that romantic (or chemical) connection I believe is necessary in order to take it to the next level. I told myself when I began Internet dating that I would be true to myself, and not do anything I felt wasn't right for me. I wish you great success in your search.*

Perhaps he really wasn't all that attractive or charming, but it doesn't hurt to be magnanimous. Rejection is painful, and no one likes to be told they're not wanted. Treat other people the way you would like to be treated. It's a rule as old as time, and it's still relevant.

There's the urban legend about men and women and rejection. A man may ask one hundred women for a date, and ninety-nine of them reject him. Because one accepts, he thinks of himself as a winner. If the same thing happened to a woman, she would believe she had been rejected ninety-nine times. Men think more of themselves that they probably should and women think less.

Ambivalence

One problem I've had is ambivalence. A few of them I was immediately sure about, but there have been several I was riding the fence about after the first brief meeting. My initial tendency was to write them off since I didn't feel the adrenaline rush immediately. My sister—my touchstone—cautioned that this was one of my patterns from the past, and suggested I give the person at least one more chance. It wouldn't have to be a long date, but perhaps another meeting longer than the first one, with me bringing my own car as before.

This isn't the Indy 500. You have to be around people to get to know them. Even though I said earlier that we shouldn't waste each other's time, we should also give someone enough time to let them shine. First dates only tell you what the person is like on a first date. It won't tell you what they would be like for the rest of your life. Because the Internet is such a rich source of singles, we tend to quickly dismiss anyone who does not immediately meet our impossibly high standards.

If you're the kind of person who can look past the obvious, so much the better. Georgia, Paula and Janine all met the same man at the same time. Jack wasn't unattractive, but he appeared to be on the nerdy side. Georgia and Paula immediately dismissed him and moved on. Janine took the time to get to know him. She discovered he was a teacher with whom she had a lot in common, a love of reading and movies among them.

Is Chemistry a Reliable Indicator of Compatibility?

I've always relied on chemistry to dictate how I feel about a man. And I've always been told by others that it was a mistake. My adrenaline only seems to rise when the man is inappropriate or unlikely to be a long-term match. Many people tell me that chemistry occurs after they've gotten to know and like someone, and I'm sure that approach works well for them.

I'm divided. It all depends on who you're talking to as to the importance of chemistry. Is it a reliable indicator of compatibility? Only sexual, probably. Try to stick out a relationship that doesn't have instant chemistry if you like the man in other ways. It could be worth the effort.

Breaking Old Patterns

I've mentioned Joseph, the accomplished athlete who competed in marathons. The one who did not smile in any of his photographs. Some people are like that, I rationalized, and it doesn't necessarily keep them from being fun-loving people.

I gave him my cellphone number, and he said he would call. The only problem was, my cellphone was new, and I didn't know how to get into my voice mail. When he finally managed to reach me, he began to lecture me about how many times he'd tried to call, how difficult I was to contact, and we had to find a better way to communicate. He droned on and on and on. I told him about the voice mail situation, and he emphatically suggested that I call my service provider immediately and find out how to obtain my voice mails. Even after I apologized for the inconvenience, he continued to lecture and cajole. He just couldn't seem to let it go.

Here's the Dear John e-mail I sent him:

After our telephone discussion Sunday, I do not
feel that we would be compatible. I don't believe
you lecturing me about the telephone situation
was productive, and I don't appreciate being
treated like a child by someone I've never even
met. I'm sure you're a nice person, but I don't
feel you are the right person for me. Thank you
for your time and good luck in your search.

The last thing I need in my life is someone who
disapproves of me. I've been getting that kind of feedback my
whole life. I had no intention of accepting it from a complete
stranger. Besides, his voice sounded like by seventy-five-year-
old uncle's.

Remember that we're trying to break away from old
patterns and try new things. Use this as an opportunity to
practice that principal.

19. Sex, Drugs and Rock & Roll

You've found them, you're having a ball, now what do you do with them? We've arrived at the editing phase of our program. We've put together the production of *Baby Boomer Bachelorette*, it looks great and is working well. But we need to do some editing. We might want to edit our profile or update our pictures.

We also have a small collection of eligible bachelors we've had a few meetings with. Now what do we do with them?

Compatibility

First, if you have more than one you're focusing on, sort them according to compatibility. Remember that the "romantic stage" of a relationship can last from three to six months (sometimes longer), depending on the individuals. During that time, our level of love chemicals is very high, and what we're experiencing is similar to what a heroin addict feels. Give this love potion time to simmer down before you leap to the next level. I'm not necessarily telling you to wait to have sex. I wouldn't wait six months to have sex with a man I liked, but remain noncommittal until your hormones have calmed down a bit. Wait until your body's not yearning for your lover twenty-four hours a day.

Overactive Stud Sensor

Don't have your "stud sensor" tuned up so high, that it passes right over a perfectly presentable, able-bodied, smart guy who might not be up to your rigid standards. Don't be looking for every little flaw a man might have just so you can throw him away for not being Mr. Perfect. Be cautious, but be generous. Measure him by the same standards you'd measure yourself.

Are you the kind of person who stays in a relationship because it is comfortable, or because the man looks like your father or your loving husband who died from a stroke last year? Do you stay with someone who belittles you, treats you like a servant or ignores you?

Partners should nurture each other, not drag each other down. That's the ideal, isn't it? While I realize the ideal situation doesn't exist, run away from a relationship that doesn't meet the needs you've selected as your most basic and important.

We're going to have some unresolved issues that keep rearing their ugly heads throughout our lives, and it's unlikely many of them will ever be resolved. What do we do about this? Accept them for what they are, and don't allow them to interfere with close physical and mental contact with a person of the opposite sex. Even though I'm still mad at my daddy for being an alcoholic and dying at an early age, I've beaten this issue *ad nauseam*. Time to just accept it, go on, and try not to find my father in another person and attempt to make the past come out differently. How do I do this? Self-acceptance and acceptance of others.

Don't Work Too Hard

Don't work too hard on your bonding with another person. When I'm with a person of the opposite sex, I'd like for it to be fun, not work. I know things aren't always going to run smoothly, and there will be issues you need to discuss. But if you're working harder on your relationship than you are at your job, then it's possibly not the right one for you—the relationship, I mean.

The coming together of a man and a woman should be exciting and adventurous. If you've been in one so long the chemistry is nonexistent, then do something that will get the adrenalin pumping again. Try taking a guided 4-wheel-drive trip over Black Bear Pass in Colorado in a four-wheel drive vehicle. That will really get your juices flowing. When it's over, you'll be so high, you'll want to copulate right there in the jeep.

It's generally understood that women are ready for sex after the man has responded to their feelings with support and understanding. Conversely (as usual), men are ready for emotional intimacy after they've had sex. I'm with the men on this one, but somehow we're going to have to learn to compromise and give the person with whom we desire to be intimate what they want.

Which brings us to the subject you've probably been
waiting for since the first paragraph of this book.

S - E - X.

Sex as a Goal

The AARP midlife survey showed that 60% of the
women and 45% of the men said they hadn't had any sex in the
last six months. (I'm assuming that's with someone other than
themselves.) That's a horrible statistic.

Sex was one of the major aims of my quest for a partner,
and it probably is yours too, or you wouldn't have been
attracted by the subtitle of this book. Like me, you probably
want to have sex at least once more before you die. Preferably
more—lots more.

What to say about sex that hasn't already been said a
thousand different times in a thousand different ways? There
are lots of things to talk about when you're discussing sex and
the Baby Boomer. We have issues that other age groups don't
have to address, like impotence, vaginal dryness, ill health,
medications, boredom—we've been doing the same things over
and over for a very long time.

I'll discuss these things, but I'm making a disclaimer
here in addition to the one at the beginning of the book. I am
not a doctor, counselor, psychologist, sex therapist, or any other
kind of "expert" on any of the subjects I've covered. If you have
a specialized problem, be sure to consult a professional for help.

Menopausal Symptoms

My circumstances may be different from the average female Baby Boomer. I became a vegetarian twelve years ago, before I reached menopause, and as a result have never suffered the menopausal symptoms my contemporaries claim to have suffered. Neither has my sister, who is fourteen months older than me, and also a vegetarian. You might chalk this up to heredity, but I remember with amazing clarity the agonies my mother endured while going through menopause. It is not hereditary.

I never had hot flashes, night sweats, lack of libido, vaginal dryness, or any of the other symptoms of which I've heard women complain. (Except excessive irritability, which I've had since I was a cheerleader in high school who didn't get asked to the football banquet, and don't consider it a menopausal symptom.)

However, I will address these symptoms since they seem to be common among a large portion of the Baby Boomer population, at least according to the ones I've interviewed and the research I've done.

First of all, do we want to have sex with the bevy of fellows we're currently sorting through, determining which ones will stay and which ones will go? If you aren't hot to trot for one or all of these guys, then it's time to go back to the computer. They're going to want to be intimate at some point, and if you don't want to, then what's the point of this little exercise? Maybe you're just looking for a buddy to go to the movies with, but I'm looking for a sex slave who also likes movies.

If I'm going to all this trouble, then I'm definitely going to have sex with them. I can go to the movies with my sister and/or my best friend. Why do I need a man for this? There's only one activity in which I would like to regularly engage for which I actually NEED a man. Note, I said *need*, not *want*. You might rather do things with a man than your girlfriends, but—unless for some reason you've formed an intimate attachment with your vibrator—you MUST have a man to have intercourse. Unless you're gay, in which case this isn't the book you should be reading. I have no experience and have done no research in that area.

Intercourse must be with a man! There's simply no way around it. So make your selection from your numerous dates, and let's get to it.

Flirting as Foreplay

Before you book a room at Motel 6, try a little flirting and judicious touching first. Get yourself all revved up and ready by stroking his hand, caressing his face, kissing the back of his neck or some other little affectionate touch that isn't necessarily sexual, but could be interpreted that way if he's into you.

How affectionate toward you is he being? I specifically asked for a man who was personable, that is, someone who wasn't afraid to touch me. I really like that in a man, and, although I'm not naturally that way, I strive to be. People respond positively to being touched. Has he held your hand when he walked you to your car? Has he put his arm around you in the movies and caressed your arm? Has he kissed you long and deeply before walking you to your door?

Speaking of kissing, guys. Do not ask a woman's permission to kiss her! Nothing is more off-putting than a guy who's too timid to take physical matters into his own hands.

Here's another thing about kissing that you may or may not agree with. Why do people open their mouths as big as they can before they kiss, then proceed to ram their tongues down each other's mouths, slathering each others lips and faces with spit? I like French kissing too, but I prefer to reserve it for someone I know well, and led up to by some judicious light kissing, gradually getting deeper as we delve into each other's passion, becoming hotter and hotter. As the moment crescendos, then ram the ol' tongue down the throat! Isn't that much better?

You've established the fact that you both want to become intimate with each other. His place or yours? Depends—which is the answer to most of your questions. Where would you feel most comfortable? Where would he feel most comfortable? If you have your newly divorced daughter and grandson living in the same house with you, and your new friend has a three thousand square foot bachelor pad, it's obvious. If you both have a houseful of children and grandchildren, rent a motel room. Like everything in this business, use common sense. If you're so enamored you've lost all sense, ask your touchstone for help.

Boomer Women in Great Sexual Shape

Remember when you were in your thirties? Authorities told us that women were in their sexual prime. Men, they said, were in their sexual prime in their twenties, and by their thirties were on the decline. We were outpacing the men in our thirties, and should have been dating men in their twenties, according to our sexual prowess.

We're facing the same thing again in our fifties, and men and women are once more in a different place. Maybe we were about the same in our forties, but I almost completely missed that decade, so you'll have to let me know.

Women in their fifties and beyond are in great shape sexually. They no longer have to worry about birth control; they are unencumbered by raising children. They're still capable of having multiple orgasms, and are more at ease with their bodies and know what they're capable of. Older women are more likely to want to experiment. Baby Boomer Babes are, in short, ready to party!

A survey conducted in New Jersey showed that 72% of women over fifty reported they had no complaints about declining sexual desire, that they were content as ever with their sex lives.

Boomer Men Have Slowed Down

Baby Boomer men have slowed down. Achieving an erection is more difficult, sometimes impossible, without direct penile stimulation. When they are aroused, their erections tend to be less firm, and their ability to maintain them is lessened.

One in four men reported being either completely or moderately impotent. These problems could be reduced or eliminated if the man in question leads a healthy lifestyle. Viagra treats the symptoms, not the problem. One solution for women would be younger men.

Perhaps this is why older men prefer younger women. They are unable to keep up sexually with us Baby Boomer ladies.

A 1999 AARP study discovered that there were 92 men for every 100 women in the age group fifty-five to sixty-four. The older we get the faster the men die off. After seventy-five, there were only 53 men for every 100 women. Better find your guy before you turn seventy-five, or better yet, go for the younger men.

Married Boomers Having a Lot of Sex

The same survey told us that so-called "senior citizens" are having sex regularly. I'm not sure how they define "seniors," but I know I received a membership application from them the day I turned fifty. Although we shy away from the senior citizen handle, we are not the least bit surprised that our compatriots way beyond fifty are just as sexually active as we'd like to be. The ones who were the most shocked were the generations younger than us, who thought we'd become so old, unattractive, sick and tired that we never even thought about sex.

There's lots of sex going on among married Baby Boomers. It has been reported that we singles are getting a lot less. Time to change all that.

Minor Children

If a man has custody of the minor children, you will most likely end up fitting yourself into his life, rather than the other way around. Your lovemaking sessions might have to be worked into the children's schedule. If the person is divorced, many child custody agreements state that neither parent can allow opposite-sex guests to stay overnight while in possession of the children. This can set up incredible barriers to overcome and should be taken into serious consideration before you become involved with someone who has minor children. It's especially difficult if they have total custody, and have sole responsibility for the kids. This doesn't happen often, but it happens. Just be sure you're ready to share your significant other with his or her children, or, vice versa, be sure they're ready to share him with you.

Overcome Guilt

Either way, don't feel guilty about taking him away from the kids. Sometimes a couple will make sex and romance the last priority with children, home, activities, elderly parents, pets and bill paying ranking before it. And if you do snatch a little time to yourselves, you or the parent may feel guilty that he's not spending this time with his kids. Get past the guilt. Everyone is entitled to spend time alone and show their love and affection for each other in a physical way. The benefits you both receive from it will translate into happier relations among the whole family.

Baby Boomers have been taught, and still believe, that self-denial is a virtue with its own rewards. While you can't afford to think only about yourself when minor children are involved, you won't be doing them any favors by denying yourself your most basic needs. You'll just end up feeling grouchy and resentful.

The Fear Barrier

What are some other barriers to great intercourse among Baby Boomers? Fear is probably the most powerful inertia-inducing feeling we have. Our fears are so varied and individual, it would be impossible to cover them all in the context of this little book. As we've discussed before, the fear of being naked is number one for women, and the inability to perform is man's biggest fear.

The first step to overcoming your fear is to admit it. Fear is universal. Concede that you're just like the rest of us. Then, understand it most likely represents some loss—dignity, power, control. Perhaps you're afraid of losing the affection of the other person, or subjecting yourself to their ridicule. Your sense of self may be challenged when you feel your body is unattractive, and you may be having one of those low self-esteem periods that plague us all.

Whatever the reason, it's not possible to completely dispel your fear. True bravery consists of doing the thing we fear in spite of it, not because we've overcome it. One of the things I'm most proud of is crossing mountain passes in a four-wheel drive vehicle. I did this in spite of the fact that I have a dreadful fear of heights which has been impossible to overcome. I've crossed those passes despite being frightened.

My sister is dreadfully afraid of flying. She just knows we're going to be hijacked by terrorists, or there will be a mechanical failure, or the weather will force us to make a crash landing. She still flies because she realizes if she ever wants to go anywhere, she'll have to drive if she refuses to fly. Usually, this would require driving across the Texas Panhandle. The Panhandle has been described by my friend, Laura, as "Hell with the fire put out." My sister wanted to do something badly enough that she stepped past the fear and did it regardless of being afraid. That is true bravery.

It's the same thing with sex and the Baby Boomer. You know you want to do it, and you know if you find somebody attractive enough, you're going to do it. Acknowledge your fear and do it anyway. Forget that youth and beauty are touted as the only deserving recipients of love and sex. Since the first Baby Boomers hit fifty, they've rejected that notion outright, and continue to have just as much sex and intimacy as any twenty-year-old.

First Encounters

My first sexual encounter was anxiety-ridden and stressful. I felt horrible about taking off my clothes—the cliche of the over-forty woman. The man didn't really look any better than I did, and he was ten years younger than me. I insisted that he keep the lights off while we made love. I explained that I had just lost a lot of weight, which was true, but I still felt uncomfortable. I wore a cute nighty that enhanced my best feature—my "big American breasts"— which made me feel a little better. The man was kind and understanding and acted as if he'd had the best sex of his life. Later, I became shameless about my body and worried about the way I looked less and less.

Anger and Depression

Anger and depression, two other deterrents to healthy middle-aged sex, should be dealt with immediately, and a health care professional should be consulted if you can't do it by yourself. Remember, though, that the first thing a psychiatrist or psychologist is going to want to do is medicate you. I would resist that as long as I possibly could. I believe in getting to the source of the problem, and taking steps to overcome it rather than take a pill to relieve the symptoms. The problem is still there if you do that.

Most drugs given for depression inhibit the libido and reduce sexual desire. You definitely do not want that.

However, my psychologist said the reason she prescribed medication was so that the patient could begin feeling better even while they were searching for the source of their unhappiness. I still declined to take medication, and have no regrets about that. You'll have to be your own judge. But don't forget what we said at the beginning of this book about respecting authority too much. You are a better judge of your body than any doctor, so don't let them browbeat you into doing something you don't want to do. Take responsibility for your own mental health.

Optimism

Even though a tendency toward optimism or pessimism seems to be inborn, scientists say optimism can be developed. If you are truly seeking a fulfilling relationship with a person of the opposite sex, then acquire some enthusiasm for life. That's another good one for having great sex when you're a Baby Boomer. Learn the art of playfulness, and you'll do fine. Everyone likes to play. Sex should be fun, not hard work.

Sex is really a function of the brain, and attitude is everything. We have ultimate control over our attitude toward the opposite sex, and whatever we decide to think or believe about them will dictate whether we have a satisfying physical relationship.

Sometimes, though, in order to have a satisfying sexual experience, we have to turn off our brains, and go with our feelings. It's often a lot more fun that way.

20. Are You Ready for Love?

Sex has been happening between two people since the first man and woman—not-very-intelligent creatures by anthropological accounts—who figured it out without reading a book. Here we are, thousands of years and millions of words later, and there are probably more books about sex than any other subject, with the possible exception of diet and exercise. I don't have any new revelations, but perhaps a refresher course would be in order.

What would it take to have a great sexual encounter besides the proper attitude? As bad as I hate to admit it, there are some changes that occur to our bodies as we age.

Boomer Bodily Changes

Obviously, women's estrogen levels drop, but that can be a good thing. Why? It increases the ratio of testosterone to female hormones, and the testosterone is the motivator for sex. Only a small percentage of women say their sex drive has fallen since they entered menopause. In fact, 10%, like me, say they had no symptoms. For the others, symptom relief is possible without drugs if we eat a healthy diet, exercise regularly and use stress-reduction techniques. We're as ready, willing and able to have sex with our partners as we ever were, probably more so.

What about men? Their testosterone levels decrease, but it's rarely enough to prevent them from continuing to have satisfying intercourse for the rest of their lives.

What about the changes in our bodies? Men don't seem to have a problem with the way they look. They think they're sexy even with a big gut hanging over their belts and their little stick legs jutting out of boxer shorts. Women don't feel the same way. We are ashamed of the way we look when we've gained weight and our varicose veins are throbbing in our legs. But, let's give the guys credit. They are much more capable of overlooking our flaws than we are. They overlook their own, and are equally generous about not noticing ours. Give yourself a break, just like your significant other does. He looks at you as if he has a soft-focus lens over his eyes.

Illness and Sex

Illness can be a great detriment to sexual function. Diabetes is a particularly nasty business and can cause all sorts of havoc in both men and women. When a man becomes diabetic, his chances of becoming impotent increase drastically. Impotence can, indeed, be a symptom of diabetes. The same disease can also cause dryness in a woman's vaginal area. Often, less sensation in the vagina can lead to difficulty in attaining orgasm.

Strokes are obvious. If you can't move, you can't have sex. Heart attacks are not uncommon among Baby Boomers. You'll be happy to know that the majority of the ones that occur while having intercourse, happen when the victim is copulating with an extramarital lover. Isn't that a great argument for fidelity? Clogged arteries keep the blood from flowing into the pelvic area the way it normally would when you're prepared to have sex, so men may be unable to achieve erections, and women may suffer loss of feeling or the ability to orgasm.

Erectile Dysfunction

By this time in their lives, Baby Boomer men have probably experienced at least one penile failure. This continues to happen more often as they age. They may not be able to have a spontaneous erection just by seeing something they would have found stimulating in their youths, such as you naked in their bed.

His erections may not be as hard, or he may not be able to maintain them for as long as he formerly did. It will take longer for him to ejaculate, or he may not be able to at all. If he does, it may not be as forceful as it once was. We need to let our men know that we cannot feel the volume of their ejaculation. They should not worry if it is less powerful. It's not a problem for us.

The predictions sound dire, and men may be horrified by this news. Remember that these are merely possibilities, and the odds can always be beaten if you're knowledgeable, and are willing to do something about it. We've already discussed at length a more healthful way of eating and the importance of exercise. They cannot be stressed enough, especially for the Baby Boomer man. As you can see, Baby Boomer women are not as drastically affected as men, so you gentlemen need to be taking much, much, better care of yourselves.

Ginkgo biloba, an herb, is said to increase the flow of blood through your body, so you might try that. But taking a pill is not going to fix things if you don't already have a healthy, fit body. Do I really need to tell you to "Quit smoking!"?

Viagra

It would be impossible to talk about Baby Boomer sex without discussing Viagra. Remember that it's a drug, just like all the other drugs doctors and pharmaceutical companies—the ultimate drug dealers—are trying to push on us. It is meant for men with erectile dysfunction, that is, the inability to get and maintain an erection.

Viagra enables men to respond to sexual stimulation. When he is sexually excited, the arteries in his penis relax and widen, thus allowing more blood to flow into the penis. The increased blood flow causes the penis to become hard and erect. The veins that normally carry blood away from the penis then become compressed. This restricts the blood flow out of the penis. With more blood flowing in and less flowing out, the penis enlarges, resulting in an erection.

The same things that clog up the blood flow to the heart and the brain do the same thing to the penis. Erectile dysfunction is caused by physical health problems, which are high blood pressure, high cholesterol, diabetes, smoking, drinking too much, or stress. All preventable. Unfortunately, thirty million men in the United States suffer from some degree of erectile dysfunction, including about half of all men aged forty to seventy. This is an incredible waste and a national shame.

Viagra increases blood flow to the penis. When the man becomes sexually aroused, he can get and maintain an erection. The man does not immediately get a hard-on when he takes the pill. He has to be sexually stimulated first. When the sexual encounter is over (he orgasms), the penis becomes flaccid as it normally would. The pill can take about thirty minutes to work and lasts up to four hours. It comes in different dose sizes which must be adjusted by a doctor. It can be taken once a day, if needed.

Men who have certain health problems are cautioned against taking Viagra. You must have a healthy heart. If you take nitrate drugs, like nitroglycerine, you should never take Viagra. It is potentially lethal.

Viagra Does Not Affect Desire!

Viagra is not an aphrodisiac for men with normal function, and it does not increase the number of orgasms a man is going to have. It does not restore libido, cure premature ejaculation, nor will it overcome an inability to ejaculate. It has been reported that Viagra will increase a man's inability to ejaculate, and he may be pounding away at the woman for the entire four hours the medicine lasts, to no avail.

Contrary to what men have led themselves to believe, having a man banging away at her for four hours is the LAST thing a woman wants. Every woman I've interviewed says the worst thing that can happen between a man and a woman sexually is for the man to take too long to orgasm. An older comedian, who said that Viagra kept him going for a long time, received this retort from his wife: "You're not drilling for oil down there, so stop it." These testimonies effectively dispel the myth that it is desirable to make love all night.

Viagra is not a solution to impotence. It is treating the symptoms, which is what all medicines do, rather than getting to the source of the problem. All the reasons why a man suffers erectile dysfunction are preventable. The prevention of the blood flow to the heart can be reversed. It can to the penis also.

Other Sex Drugs

Levitra is close to Viagra, the difference being that it lasts up to twenty-fours. The side effects are similar to Viagra. Cialis allegedly lasts up to thirty-six hours, and it's not affected by food. As is true with Viagra, neither of these drugs will fix nerve damage caused by end-stage diabetes or prostate removal surgery or impotence caused by psychological problems. And they do not affect desire.

The development of drugs for men has proliferated because scientists understand the mechanics of the male erection. The news for women is not so good. Our sexuality is allegedly more complicated than men's and merely improving circulation is probably not going to do much good. Until there is an understanding of the female physiology, there probably won't be any truly effective drugs for female sexual dysfunction.

Other Ways of Maintaining Sexual Prowess

There are other ways of maintaining your sexual prowess. Think about satisfying the woman you're with rather than thinking of sex as strictly satisfying your own needs. Taking the focus off one's self always enables us to relax and perform better. Good news for all Baby Boomers: the more sex you have, the better. It improves your confidence and your performance.

Vaginal Dryness

More sex is the answer to women's vaginal dryness also. If you don't have a partner yet, buy some sort of penis-shaped sex toy, and use that to keep yourself lubricated. Don't turn your nose up when I say that. Nobody will know about it but you. Don't you ever watch "The Sunday Night Sex Show"? That lady is way past her sixties, and she's talking about sex like she's a pro.

Avoid anything that causes dryness such as antihistamines or diuretics. Don't drink alcohol or coffee. Very dehydrating. You won't need stimulants if you're following the energy-enhancing diet I recommended. Drink lots of water and eat more soy products, which have been shown to add moisture to the vaginal walls. Add water-based foods to your diet like—here it comes—fruits and vegetables!

Do I really need to say, USE A CONDOM? Especially the first few months. Ask your friend to voluntarily get an HIV test, and the two of you go together. Then you'll both feel better. Go to the pharmacy and buy some condoms right now, long before you've even thought about going to bed with him. You might be able to wait for the eventual sexual history discussion, but I couldn't.

Now, we're all hard and wet and ready for the real thing. We don't want to just jump in bed and go at it. This requires a little build-up, a little finesse.

Flirting

How about a little flirting with your intended partner? It's much more stimulating to take his arm as you're walking into the restaurant, kiss her cheek after you pull the chair out for her, put your hand on his thigh while he's driving the car. Stimulate each other through sight, sound and touch before you get down to the nitty gritty. Put on a sexy outfit for him, take her to a movie that's romantic and sexually arousing, make prolonged eye contact over a picnic lunch, exchange clever, verbal repartee with a sexual connotation. Break out of whatever box you've placed yourself into and do something out of character. Tease and play and work up to the final act.

Nothing is more boring than those movies where the characters strip off their clothes and have sex, without any sexual tension or build-up. Give me sexual tension any day! Don't just touch each other when you intend to have sex.

Foreplay

What about foreplay? What about the sexual things that usually proceed intercourse. Kissing, hugging, touching, feeling, talking—take as long as you want. It's not necessary to have sex the first time.

I'm hoping everyone reading this is a regular masturbator. I'm sure you guys are. I don't think men need to be told it's healthy and fun. You women probably do, though. But what about doing it in front of him? Should you touch yourself? Quite frankly, I'm sure the man would love it. In fact, I know he would. Every man I interviewed said he would not only NOT mind if a woman touched herself, he'd be turned on by it.

Fantasizing

Is fantasizing cheating? If you're thinking about Vin Diesel while you're straddling Average Joe, does it mean you're unfaithful to Joe? Don't be ridiculous. Everybody does this, and it is a great simulator to ecstatic sex. Making love with somebody other than your partner is the number one fantasy for lovers of all sexes and ages. We'll probably be dreaming about Jude Law, and he'll be seeing Pamela Anderson. In our fantasies we'll still be thirty years old. It doesn't mean we want to have sex with these people, it just means we have healthy libidos and it's enhancing our present relationship.

I dated an identical twin named Rory whose brother I had lusted after for years (he was married). Every time I had sex with Rory, I fantasized he was his brother. But he never knew that and was never hurt by it. He was probably fantasizing about my sister while he made love to me.

Guys, don't believe for a second women don't think about sex as much as you do. It's been estimated that 10%-20% of women (myself included) have the equivalent of male "wet dreams." That is, we have orgasms while we sleep. We're thinking about sex when we're not even conscious.

Why Are Baby Boomer Women Having Sex?

We're not having sex for the same reasons women under thirty-five are having it. A recent study discovered that 61% of women under thirty-five were having sex for "love." For women between thirty-six and fifty-seven, only 38% said that love had anything to do with it.

Men, as usual, were just the opposite. Only 31% of the under thirty-five males claimed they had sex primarily for "love," but—shocker of shockers—more than half of the older men said they had sex for that reason. The point is, Baby Boomer women are hot to trot, and it doesn't necessarily have to be with someone they're in love with. They also placed a higher priority on other sexual pleasures, such as swimming in the nude or watching X-rated videos than younger women. What are you guys waiting for? We are ready!

Oral Sex

I'll go down on you if you'll go down on me. I asked the aforementioned twin what he considered the most erotic thing a woman could do. He said a woman getting off while giving him a blow job was the biggest turn-on he had ever experienced. I sincerely hope he wasn't expecting that to happen with me.

Some women really get into performing fellatio, and some don't. I find going down on a man a performance I reserve for the most beloved of fellows. I receive pleasure from seeing him very, very happy, and I certainly admire a well-formed penis as much as the next woman. I don't actually get-off on it (have an orgasm), so if you're getting it from me, you're a lucky guy.

Most men I talked with said they enjoyed cunnilingus. I'm willing to take their word for it. I've heard that men enjoy blow jobs so much because it's a purely unselfish act. You could say the same thing about them going down on us, though some women have to have this performed on them in order to have an orgasm. That's a whole other subject, and in the bibliography, I refer you to some books about sex and the problem of women's inability to have orgasm during sexual intercourse.

If you like the guy, and you know he's clean, give him a blow job. He'll be grateful. The top one-third (head and coronal ridge) of the penis is the most sensitive part—that's some good information to have. In order to give him the most pleasure, concentrate your efforts there. According to my sources, the seam running down the underside of the penis is the only part of the shaft that's really sensitive. I guess they're saying don't waste your time anywhere else.

When a man performs cunnilingus on a woman, the labia are quite sensitive, but the manipulation of the clitoris is what makes the woman orgasm. This can be done with the finger first, and then the mouth, tongue and teeth.

Of course, there are tons of other things you can do to arouse and stimulate the other person, but these are beyond the scope of this book. There's plenty of information out there, so go look for it if you think you don't know enough about sex after all these years. If there's anything truly new, I haven't found it. You'll probably be just as well off relying on your memory and instincts.

Intercourse

Once you're both ready for entry, the woman probably having had at least one orgasm from cunnilingus, you can pick whichever position seems appropriate. Most people start with the male superior position.

Penile insertion will not automatically bring a woman to orgasm. Surely everyone knows by now that a woman requires clitoral stimulation in order to orgasm. The penis in the male superior position is not in a position to give the kind of stimulation she needs. It would be appropriate at this point for the man to manually stimulate her clitoris, or for the woman to do it herself. It is more effective for the woman to do it, as she knows exactly what type and how much pressure is needed, Touching herself is a real turn-on for the man. It's a win-win situation.

Jane Juska's book, *A Round Heeled Woman*, was a revelation regarding the wants, needs and sexual desires of a sixty-seven year old woman. She placed an ad in the personals of the *New York Review of Books*, stating that she would like to have a lot of sex with a man she liked. Very brave for a woman with little experience.

After reading her book, and finding out about the men she met up with, I ran screaming to my sister. To say her choices were limited would be a colossal understatement. Much of this, however, may be attributed to the type of ad she posted. She got what she advertised for. The same will hold true for your profile, which is why it's important to make it expressive of your needs and wants

I mention Juska's book because, while it was interesting, entertaining and well-written, she subscribed to the myth of the vaginal orgasm. She seemed to expect, still thought it possible, that a woman's vagina could orgasm independent of the clitoris. Let me clear this up. *All female orgasms originate with the clitoris.* There is no such thing as the vaginal orgasm. You may feel as if there is, when your senses all seem to be exploding. But women need to quit striving for something that doesn't exist and quit feeling inadequate when they are unable to achieve it.

Female superior puts the woman in a position to receive the most direct clitoral stimulation, but she may still need or want to touch herself.

The rear-entry position has been suggested by the experts as an excellent position for mid-life partners. As the woman's chest lies on the bed, the position tends to elongate her vaginal barrel. This happily creates a much tighter fit for the man's penis, causing his erection to feel bigger and stronger to both of them. She can also stimulate herself this way or the man can do it for her.

Allow yourself to be swept away by passion. Let go of your control and let things happen at whatever pace feels good to both of you. To add spark and excitement, keep your eyes open during lovemaking, or at least open them during certain points. Making eye contact while engaging in oral sex or during orgasm will bring a feeling of connectedness to your passion, and will be exciting and stimulating.

Loss of Erection

If the man loses his erection, don't make a big deal out of it. Don't try to get it back again by frantically giving him oral sex or manually stimulating his penis. Just let it go. Don't make a fuss over him, but don't say it doesn't matter. Just ignore the situation. Pretend it didn't happen. It will come back again.

The man should concentrate on satisfying his partner rather than worrying about his erection. Guys, a woman can be satisfied by a partial erection, so it's not the end of the world.

Many times when I was a young woman, and the man had ejaculated before I achieved orgasm, I was still able to use his penis inside me to bring myself to orgasm, sometimes with a little help from my or his fingers.

Loss of an erection is not anyone's fault. Not the man's nor the woman's, so don't blame your partner.

Once you've completed the act to both partner's satisfaction—we hope—then the afterglow sets in. Your body has created a chemical called "oxytocin," and it makes you feel

Show quality, not quantity.

all warm and cuddly. Women produce more oxytocin than men do. That's why the men are more capable of turning over and going straight to sleep without a snuggling session.

My Theory of the Cure for Infidelity

Whether the mother is a human or a non-human animal, oxytocin is produced when she has a baby. It is nature's way of bonding her to the infant so she will think taking care of it is the most desirable thing in the world. Then she won't abandon the little tyke in the woods.

I guess that's the way we're supposed to feel about our sex partners, too. They're so wonderful, we'd never abandon them in the forest. I wonder if I've just figured out why men tend to cheat on their partners more than women do? Could it be the absence of oxytocin? Could a remedy for this be oxytocin injections for men? I think some research needs to be done on this. It could be the cure for infidelity.

We should be feeling terrific by now. Sex relieves tension, elevates mood and strengthens the immune system. Wow! All this and orgasm too?

POSTPRODUCTION

♀

21. Afterglow

*B*aby Boomer Bachelorette—the Miniseries is over. The curtain has fallen, and the nightly news is on the tube. Our production has come to an end, and it's time to assess if it was successful or not.

Postproduction Follow-Up

We call this phase the "Postproduction Follow-Up." There is still much work to be done. We need to check our ratings, so to speak, and see if we accomplished all our goals. Were the results what we expected?

You're basking in the afterglow of orgiastic ecstasy, and you're thinking he may be the ONE. What do you want to do about that? Let's assume he thinks the same thing, too. Is marriage the inevitable conclusion to all this effort? It was for Trista and Ryan, but what about you?

Marriage or Living Together?

It depends on what you decided from the beginning you were looking for. If love and marriage are what you ultimately want, and you're sure this is the right thing, then do it. Remember, however, that marriage ends all possibilities. Ask yourself this question: "Can someone be funny enough, horny enough and faithful enough for the next fifty years to keep me happy?"

There's no reason, however, why you can't date until the day you die. There's no law that says you have to get married just because you're having sex with someone. If you're suited to the marriage state—and some of us are better at it than others—and you're happy being a couple and pooling your financial resources, then marriage is a good way to go.

Some women have told me that they don't want to be alone. Unless you marry a man significantly younger than you, he will most likely die first, and you will be alone again. That's just the way it is.

Past evidence points to the fact that I don't function well in the marital state. I married the wrong man for the wrong reasons. I'm optimistic, though. A new marriage might be much better. I'm not sure about that, so I'm probably a candidate for dating until I'm one hundred or older. Besides, dating can be lots of fun!

Do not tell him you love him after the first week! This is a fatal error, and one many women commit. I would advise waiting for a length of time determined by your touchstone even if he's said he loved you. If he says it to you within the first month, be suspicious. Give it some time before you utter those commitment words.

Everyone needs to be validated. Everyone needs to know that their significant other honors and approves of them. Be generous with your support and enthusiasm. It will be rewarded by the same things coming back to you.

It's Not Personal?

What if your new relationship begins to grow a little stale? What if he says he "needs his space," those dreaded words uttered by everyone who is searching for an excuse to take the first exit off the relationship freeway. The wayward partner tells us not to take it personally. Who of us hasn't heard the words, "It's not personal"?

What? He's breaking up with you, so since when is it not personal? When that happens, your best bet is to let it go. He may not want or need what you have to offer, but you've already learned that there are others out there who do. Try not to cling or whine or hold onto his leg while he drags you out the front door. Let go!

Dried-Up Options

What if you haven't found someone compatible, and all your possibilities seem to have dried up? You're not getting that many e-mails from interested guys. You feel as if you've been through all the men on the website you've chosen. At this point you need to broaden your horizons. For instance, when you search for men, reduce or increase your height requirement by an inch. I requested men between 5'10" and 6'4". When I decided I needed more responses, I lowered my height requirement to 5'9". You could increase the geographical area you want searched from fifty miles to one-hundred miles.

Making small changes in your search parameters will bring more interesting men to your notice. If you feel as if you've expanded your options as far as you're willing to, now would be the time to considering either moving to another dating website or adding another one to your repertoire. Robin De Luca, the "Cyber-Dating Guru," says that at one time she was signed up with as many as five dating websites. Since she's very pretty and probably received many responses, I think she must have had a date every night.

Starting Over

Begin the process all over again. Think of it as a new beginning. You're more experienced now. Your self-confidence is much greater than it was the day you had that first date. Plan a new production. Analyze what went wrong with this one if, indeed, anything went wrong. Avoid those same pitfalls the next time.

Judging by all the dating websites on the Internet, you won't have any trouble finding someone else, no matter how old you are. There is apparently a website that covers every age, lifestyle, and kinky activity in the universe. I saw one on TV that caters to people who like to pretend they're horses. No, I'm not kidding. They wear bridles, harnesses, and one woman even wore a pair of hooves fashioned for her hands and feet. So don't despair, pony girl. You'll be dating again in no time.

When You're Tired, Frustrated or Overwhelmed

If you get too tired or frustrated or overwhelmed or scared, put it on hold for a few months. This can be an all-consuming project, and you may short circuit during the process. There's no law that says you have to pursue this twenty-four hours a day. Give it a rest, a long one, if you need to. I took a break to reassess my "production," or what I referred to as "Postproduction Follow-Up." I made a few changes to my approach, rested, thought about other things, and completed a number of projects. Refreshed, I went back to it, ultimately achieving even better results. There's no timeline for love. It can happen any time.

The End of the Series

You've probably watched enough TV series to realize that once the couple get together, i.e., have sex, form a loving relationship and get married, the series is over. Who wants to watch *Remington Steele* when they're married, or *Who's the Boss*, or *The Nanny*, or *Moonlighting*? Our show is over. Baby Boomer Bachelorette is preparing for the sequel. It's time to go to bed.

Before we are able to sleep, however, there is one nagging question left unanswered. How did our heroine fare with the hero when she told him her real age? That she was a number of years older than her profile indicated? Was he so angry that she lied that he never wanted to see her again? How would you feel if a man with whom you were highly compatible told you he was older than he'd originally claimed?

Didn't Sean Penn forgive Elizabeth McGovern in *Racing with the Moon* when he found out she'd been deceiving him about being rich? Didn't Ralph Fiennes still love Jennifer Lopez when he discovered she was really just a maid in *Maid in Manhattan*?

Remember these few words of wisdom, carry them with you, and apply them to all your endeavors.

**Persistence is the key to success.
Failure only happens when you give up.**

Good luck and happy dating!

Appendix

Recommended Reading

General Interest

Juska, Jane, *A Round-Heeled Woman*, New York: Villard, 2003.

Morris, Barbara, *Putting Old on Hold*, Escondido, CA: Image F/X, 2001.

Null, Gary, Ph.D., with Koestler, Vicki Riba, *The Baby Boomer's Guide to Getting It Right the Second Time Around*, New York: Carroll & Graf Publishers, Inc. 2001.

Pogrebin, Letty Cottin, *Getting Over Getting Older*, Berkeley Books, 1996.

Sheehy, Gail, *New Passages*, New York: Random House, 1995.

Dating and Relationships

Blake, Tom, *Middle Aged and Dating Again*, Dana Point, CA: Tooter's Publishing, 1997, 2nd Ed. 2001.

Brings, Felicia and Winter, Susan, *Older Women, Younger Men: New Options for Love and Romance*, New Horizon Press, 2000.

De Luca, Robin, *The Cyber-Guru's Guide to Online Dating*, 2003.

Harrison, Barbara, *50+ and Looking for Love Online*, Freedom, CA: The Crossing Press, 2000.

Solomon, Alice, *Find the Love of Your Life After Fifty!*, Writers' Collective, 2003.

Zuckerman, Rachelle, *Young at Heart: The Mature Woman's Guide to Finding and Keeping Romance*, McGraw-Hill/Contemporary Books, 2001

Diet and Exercise

Vedral, Joyce L., Ph.D., *Bone-Building/Body-Shaping Workout*, Fireside, 1998.

Vedral, Joyce L., Ph.D., *Definition*, Warner Books, 1995.

Vedral, Joyce L., Ph.D., *Fat-Burning Workout*, Warner Books, 1991.

Vedral, Joyce L., Ph.D., *Weight Training Made Easy*, Warner Books, 1997.

Westcott, Wayne L. and Baechle, Thomas R., *Strength Training Past 50*, Human Kinetics, 1998.

Sex

Berman, Jennifer, M.D., Berman, Laura, Ph.D., and Bumiller, Elisabeth (Contributor), *For Women Only: A Revolution Guide to Overcoming Sexual Dysfunction and Reclaiming Your Sex Life*, Henry Holt & Company, Inc., 2001.

Block, Joe D., Pd.D., with Bakos, Susan Crain, *Sex Over 50*, Paramus, NJ: Reward Books, 1999.

Hutchins, D. Claire, *Five Minutes to Orgasm Every Time You Make Love*, Grand Prairie, TX: JPS Publishing Company, 1998, 2nd Ed. 2000.

Resources

Baby Boomer Internet Dating Services

Senior Friend Finder
Seniors Circle
Third Age Connections

Other Websites

www.boomerwomenspeak.com
www.curvesinternational.com
www.cyberdatingguru.com
www.e-cyrano.com
www.gorgeousgrandma.com
www.profiledoctor.com
www.soulmatepics.com
www.singleshots.com
www.weightwatchers.com
www.allocate.com/dating-sites/United_States

Newsletters

Ourselves: Women at the Center of Life—Amy Lynch, publisher and editor

Index